Harry E Towne

MW00988886

# THE CHURCH THAT DARED TO CHANGE

## Michael R. Tucker

**TYNDALE**
House Publishers, Inc.
Wheaton, Illinois

COVERDALE
House Publishers, Ltd.
London, England

To Nancy

Library of Congress Catalog Card Number 74-21971
ISBN 8423-0280-8
Copyright © 1975 by Tyndale House Publishers, Inc.,
Wheaton, Illinois 60187. All rights reserved.
First printing, January 1975
Printed in the United States of America

# CONTENTS

# FOREWORD

*Vernon C. Grounds, Ph.D., Th.D.*
*President, Conservative Baptist*
*Theological Seminary*

Through the centuries since Pentecost, God has been building his church by gifting it with Spirit-endowed leaders, especially pastor-teachers. Michael Tucker is one of God's choice gifts to the church of Jesus Christ today. Under his biblically oriented ministry, a dying fellowship of believers on the verge of disbanding has experienced a sort of resurrection. Within only a few years Temple Baptist Church in Colorado Springs has become one of the most exciting, dynamic centers of Christian teaching, outreach, and service in our entire state. Though its growth statistically has been rapid and extraordinary, the more significant aspect of that growth has occurred in the lives of people who have been discovering that they too are gifted and have a ministry.

As pastor-in-residence at Conservative Baptist Seminary during the fall of 1973, the youthful author of this book ignited our students, urging them to view the ministry of the local church as the greatest opportunity for creative investment of one's life and talents. May the reading of this account of a transformed church trigger the transformation of many other churches.

# PREFACE

Any attempt to add to the "church renewal" books available today must be well defined. Much of the material on the market has been produced by theoreticians. Teachers have told "how to do it." That is good. Theory is necessary. But lately the trend has been, "This is how it happened."

Almost all of these "success stories" have one factor in common: the pastor started the church or began his ministry there when the church was tiny. That situation has the distinct advantage that new people knew what they were getting into when they identified with that church. The pastor's "radical" ideas were acceptable to people *before* they associated themselves with that church.

The problem is that most pastors do not start churches. Most church renewal *must* take place in established churches with varying lengths of history.

What has happened at Temple Baptist Church in Colorado Springs thus differs from what has happened at Circle Church in Chicago, Coral Ridge Presbyterian in Fort Lauderdale, and Our Heritage Wesleyan Church in Scottsdale. Temple had twenty years of ups and downs before God was ready to

accomplish his work there. Only a few months before God began renewal, the church had dismissed
its pastor. There was bitterness and a vicious battle.
Many people left. A candidate was brought to interview for the available pastorate. The vote was more
than a majority to call him but less than the three-
fourths required to hire a pastor. Again there was
infighting. More left. The rejected candidate
started his own church in the city and took about a
third of the members with him.

The church was going under for the third time.
The leaders were bruised and discouraged. Pri-
vately they agreed to shut the doors, sell the property, and disperse any remaining funds to missionaries.

Then God reversed the total trend of the
church. Temple didn't die. Instead, it was renewed
by God's Spirit working in its people. Here is how
renewal happened in a dying church that dared to
change. This volume is written to encourage pastors, church leaders, and all Christians that the same
thing could happen in many other churches.

# 1

## What's Happened

**Most important of all, continue to show deep love for each other, for love makes up for many of your faults.**

1 Peter 4:8
[The Living Bible]

"To love means to seek the highest good of the person loved." That definition is not exhaustive. In fact, it is technically poor since it uses a derivative of the word being defined. Nonetheless, that oversimplified definition of love solves lots of problems and answers many questions.

Peter points out that love is prerequisite to all else. It must come "before" (Greek: *pro*) *all* things. In the church, love should precede program. It is not possible to create love and its results by keeping people busy in activity. Love must be *before* all things. Simply getting people "involved" is not the answer. Love is the answer. When there is genuine love among Christians, genuine God-motivated activity results.

Paul explains in 1 Corinthians 13 and Galatians 5 that love is the foundation of God's work among Christian people. The fruit of the Spirit in Galatians 5:22, 23 is based on love. The other manifestations of that fruit (joy, peace, patience, kindness, goodness, faithfulness, gentleness, self-control) can be built only upon the solid foundation of seeking the highest good of the other person. Without love, Paul writes, we are just a loud noise. Even though our doctrine is straight and our actions are commendable, without love we have missed the point.

Love encourages more love. People often wrongly define love as getting. The simple definition above, however, shows that love means giving. In premarital counseling I always ask couples the question: "Why do you want to be married to the person seated next to you?" Very often the answer is: "Because I love him/her." Then I solicit an explanation of their meaning of love. Frequently the person will define the concept as "He makes me feel good," or "I enjoy being with him," or "I'm happiest when we're together." All these ideas miss the mark. All these statements define love as getting, not giving.

Even married people usually define love as getting: "I'll love you if you will love me in return." But the Bible says that Christians should love one another *before* all things. It is an amazing discovery to many people that when we love, we receive love in return—not always immediately and not all the time, but it happens. Francis Schaeffer has pointed out from John 13:34, 35 that loving other Christians is the mark of a Christian; that is how the world will know that we belong to Jesus (*The Church at the End of the 20th Century,* p. 133).

In the 1 Peter 4 passage we learn that love hides sins. Peter does not intend to imply that sins are hidden from God, or that we need not confess our faults. What he says in the context is that love does not drag another's faults into the spotlight. Christians are not to be critical or picky with each other. We are supposed to overlook each other's faults. We should be willing to forgive each other (even if not asked to do so by the offender), think the best of each other, and refrain from accusing the brethren—which, by the way, is Satan's job (Revelation 12:10).

This is what has happened at Temple: love. God has given the Christians in Colorado Springs love for one another. Love came first. It came from the Word. It came before programs, activity, buildings, and excitement. It came from a background of in-fighting, bitterness, and church splits.

Objective love for one another is not drippy sentimentalism, but it does include emotionalism. Care, concern, and unity in the Body are based on love. No one at Temple tells Christians to love one another. They just do. No one tells anyone to visit the sick and elderly. They just do. Church members have almost always visited other members in the hospital before any of the pastors at Temple learns that one of the flock is in need. Members show concern by praying for one another. Baby-sitting and meals taken to people in need are common. Sharing one's life takes time, but that is what love is: taking time for others.

Love has created the increase. Before renewal began, Temple averaged 124 people in Sunday school each week and 137 in the morning service. Now, just a little over three years later, we have an average of over 400 in Sunday school and 600 in the morning services. The Sunday evening service has climbed from an average of 87 to over 300, frequently with 400 in the service. The physical growth is without contests, prizes, gimmicks, or busing. There is no "rally day," "bring-a-friend day," or "pack-a-pew night." The growth is honest, solid growth.

In the same period of time the annual budget has risen from $26,000 to $100,000. Annual Missions giving has jumped from $5,000 to $22,000.

The real evidence of renewal is not in physical growth, but in lives. People who have been satisfied for years to warm pews on Sunday morning are now engaged in the work of the ministry. Spiritual growth and changed lives are evident everywhere. There is no prodding "to get involved"; Christians just do. Working from people to program has allowed fresh approaches to long-held biblical concepts. New programs die and others begin almost overnight. The church is alive and enthusiastic. Visitors as well as members know it when they walk in the door. Its atmosphere is not prostituted by loud high pressure, preaching, or a frenzied song service. The attitude of love just saturates the Body, overflows, and immerses all who get close.

# 2

## What God Used

God has given each of you some special abilities; be sure to use them to help each other, passing on to others God's many kinds of blessings.

1 Peter 4:10 [TLB]

People don't like simple answers. But the explanation to church renewal at Temple is simple. Frankly, I am sometimes embarrassed at ministers' meetings when people ask, "What are you doing in Colorado Springs to cause such excitement, change, and growth?" I usually choke up, perspire heavily, and try to dodge the question with a trite remark. The real answer is simplistic. It's not usually acceptable. It sounds crazy to some, super-pious to others. Christian educators tell us that 10-15 percent growth per year is good. Temple grows at the rate of 50 percent per year. Here are the reasons:

# 1. GOD'S SOVEREIGNTY

After all is examined and explained, God's sovereignty must be recognized as the major factor. The pastor at Temple is the same man who has pastored elsewhere, and church renewal did not take place there. The people of Temple are the same ones who have been in that church or others for years, and renewal did not take place. The new converts at Temple hadn't even heard the term before. They didn't cause renewal. The final explanation must be that God decided to move and bless. And he did. Of course, there is no answer to the question of why God does what he does. He is God. We don't ask his motives. We simply obey and cooperate. We may not understand, but he never asked us to understand.

God has put together a unique combination of people, leaders, situation, and burdens to create an explosive church. The summer ministries of field trips and camp outs, the coffeehouse ministry, the home Bible studies, the singles' ministries, the choirs, the educational ministries have all met needs and grown. God opens up and shuts down ministries. He sovereignly does his work.

## 2. GROWTH OF THE CITY

Growth of the city cannot be ignored. Colorado Springs is one of the fastest growing cities in the nation. Many businesses and institutions grow rapidly beneath Pikes Peak. When people move they are prepared for changes in many areas of life. A newcomer in a new neighborhood is ripe for outreach. New people in the city are seeking new friends. They have special social needs. God has used this situation to cause church growth.

This factor is not the full answer, however. A great number of churches in Colorado Springs aren't growing at all. And very few are booming like Temple. Even the gimmicks and prizes that others offer aren't doing the job in some instances. Those who do extensive busing aren't experiencing the same rate of growth.

Temple is not built on an extensive visitation program. Each new arrival receives a letter from the pastor welcoming him to the city (see Letter 1 in Appendix). The suggestion is made in the letter that perhaps God has a purpose for moving the newcomer's life to our city. We offer to help the person as he makes adjustments to his new environment. But the newcomer is not visited in his home unless he makes some contact with the church. Temple majors on outreach to those whom God has already prepared. There is no door-to-door visitation or canvassing in any neighborhood. We don't believe that approach reaches people in an effective way in our situation. Better ways exist to help people and introduce them to Christ.

## 3. EXPOSITORY PREACHING

"Verse-by-verse Bible teaching for your life today," proclaims our newspaper ad. The Bible is systematically taught. The preaching is exposition. Almost always the Sunday morning and evening and the midweek services are verse-by-verse book studies. The whole concept of spiritual growth lies here. We believe that Christians love and minister when they grow in Christ. *The only way to grow is through study of God's written Word.* We at Temple make no apologies for that dogmatic statement. Its truth is evident throughout our church. Christians who have sat for years under topical, surface preaching have "come alive" under exposition of the Scriptures. Hundreds of people testify that they have been active church members for years, but never really grew in their spiritual lives until they were exposed to expository preaching.

John Killinger said: "People are not tired of preaching, but of non-preaching, of the badly garbled, anachronistic, irrelevant drivel that has in so many places passed for preaching because there was no real preaching to measure it against" (*The Centrality of Preaching*, p. 21).

Expository preaching is defined by Prof. Haddon Robinson of Dallas Theological Seminary as "the proclamation of a biblical concept derived from an historical-grammatical study of a passage in its context which the Holy Spirit has first made vital in the personality of the preacher and through him applies accurately in the experience of the congregation."

People don't attend church on Sunday to hear someone's views on the world situation. They aren't interested in a rerun of the week's headlines or the six o'clock news. They want to know if God has a word for their lives. They scratch and fight all week to stay on top of sin and temptation. (So please, preacher, give them some help from the Book God wrote. Don't waste their time. Help them.)

Homiletical hopscotch may be biblical preaching but it doesn't meet people's need to learn what God says. Topical preaching, preaching on themes, tends to carry the weight of the preacher's word, not God's Word. If the preacher is interesting, people may remember what he said, but they won't know what the Bible says. Topical preaching tends to be superficial. The preacher doesn't usually stay in one passage long enough to wrestle with the deep and honest questions of the text. Expository preaching is more than using one passage for a "jumping-off place" so the preacher can say what he wants to say. The outline and content of the message must emerge *from* the passage, not be imposed *on* the passage. The writer's intent in the passage is the crux of the message from any portion of Scripture.

This approach to preaching takes time, lots of time. My personal preparation requires fifteen to twenty hours per message. Charles Haddon Spurgeon advised his students, "Spare neither labor in the study, prayer in the closet, nor zeal in the pulpit" (*Lectures to My Students,* p. 345). Obviously the preacher must discipline his day to spend that amount of time on sernıon preparation. But the priority is clearly presented in Peter's imperative to church leaders, "Feed the flock of God" (1 Peter 5:2).

Already you recognize that the pastor who invests so much time in sermon preparation must be in a church where either (1) many parts of the ministry are neglected, or (2) many people share the ministry. For a pastor to devote time to studying, the congregation must understand that their lives are enriched through the results of his preparation. This concept implies that the pastor *cannot* be involved in many areas traditionally dumped into his lap. For instance, I do very little visitation. One or two nights a month is all I can afford. I meet and minister to people who have enough need to make an appointment and come to my office. We have people into our home on Sundays and Wednesdays after church. I meet with men for lunch almost every day. But I do no door-to-door visitation. I visit and counsel with certain individuals, and call upon a few people who visit our church. I do try to see all who are hospitalized. My priorities based on the Word demand that approach. Other large areas of administration never concern me. Buildings and maintenance are completely cared for by the church leaders. Frequently rather large changes are made in the church plant without my knowledge. Recently the church bought an 11,636 square-foot office building next door. One floor required complete remodeling for our use. The men of the church supervised the whole project. My contact with the project was only as an observer. I seldom even met with the committee responsible for the endeavor.

Another implication of the principle of expository preaching in our situation is that most evangelism takes place outside the building. The church services are primarily "for the perfecting of the saints, for the work of the ministry, for the edifying of the body of Christ" (Ephesians 4:12).

The gospel is always presented, but admittedly in capsule form. There are never any evangelistic meetings inside the church's walls. The whole concept is that as Christians are built up in the faith, and equipped to do the work of the ministry, they will grow and respond to God's Word. In a natural overflow of the Christian life, they will share God's good news with others. At Temple we reject the idea that the pastor is the only one qualified to lead people to Christ. So often Christians who want their friends to come to Christ take them to church where they will hear an evangelistic sermon and be persuaded to respond to an altar call. How much greater the joy for a Christian to be equipped to win his friend to Christ at home, then bring the new convert to church where he will receive help for his spiritual life and also be equipped to reproduce.

Many Christians at Temple give evidence that they sat under "gospel preaching" for years and never grew. The way of salvation was explained and explained and explained. The Word was never taught. They sat, were bored, and finally left.

Certainly the New Testament commands the church to evangelize. But there is no hint that evangelism should take place in church meetings. We have discovered that evangelism outside the building causes more people to accept their responsibility to share Christ.

Evangelism takes place through our home Bible studies, coffeehouse, college campus workers, and campground singers. Our people are trained and encouraged to witness wherever they are. Evangelism takes place in parks, offices, and homes. Men's evangelistic luncheons and dinners are held. The vehicles for evangelism are numerous. This approach allows the church services to center on the teaching of God's Word for God's people.

## 4. SHARED MINISTRY

Every believer has a spiritual gift (I Corinthians 12:7). At Temple we encourage each Christian to discover his gifts and use them in the ministry God has given him. For years the church has allowed the clergy to do the work of the ministry while most Christians watch. This practice has resulted in three unfortunate situations: (1) *A discouraged clergy.* No man can do all the work of the ministry in a local church. It is well known that many ministers are leaving the parish ministry. A survey of one denomination revealed that half of its pastors have "seriously considered leaving the parish ministry." Seminarians frequently don't even consider the local church ministry as a viable option. Many pastors are discouraged and pessimistic. (2) *Carnal Christians.* By allowing the pastor to do all the work of the ministry in the church the remainder of the Body is robbed of its growth through service. Churches are full of Christians who pledge allegiance to the pastor, but who aren't growing spiritually simply because they aren't encouraged to do the work of the ministry. They are faithful to the institution, but they've never heard that they have spiritual gifts to develop. (3) *An unevangelized world.* Frankly, the approach of the "pastor only" doing the work of the ministry is not successful. The world is not being dented for Christ.

We have discovered, however, that sermons and lessons and books on spiritual gifts don't fully meet the need of helping individuals to discover their gifts. In addition to these methods, it is essential that every Christian be confronted one-on-one. Every Christian at Temple for any length of time has heard from the Word that he has a spiritual gift. He has undoubtedly considered what his gift may be.

But *usually* he won't come to a firm conviction until another Christian helps him personally. Our approach is through the elders.

Our elders have no policy-making authority or responsibility. They simply minister to people. Each elder has twelve to fourteen family units under his care. He is responsible to minister to these people. He calls them regularly and shares prayer requests with them and asks for their requests. He is available for counsel and advice. His group of families meets only a few times per year as a group. The elders have no officers and rarely meet as a whole group. The pastor does meet with all the elders bimonthly, however, in groups of three or four. Part of an elder's responsibility is to speak with *each* individual in his group about his personal spiritual gifts. This approach assures that *every* member of the church will be challenged on a one-to-one basis to discover and use his spiritual gift.

People are encouraged to find their gifts by:

(1) Knowing the lists of gifts in Romans 12, Ephesians 4, and 1 Corinthians 12. We believe there are other gifts beyond those listed, however.

(2) Asking the question, "What do I enjoy doing in the ministry?"

(3) Trying several different ministries.

(4) Seeking the advice of another spiritually mature Christian. Sometimes others can see our gifts more quickly than we can.

(5) Noticing what works. The fruit borne is not the only criterion, but it is a valid one.

(6) Being filled with the Holy Spirit. Any true Christian who seeks God's will in his life and earnestly wants to know his spiritual gift, will find it. God is not hiding the facts. He wants to show every believer what his supernatural ability is.

Sharing the ministry must be more than a theory. People must see and believe that the ministry is truly shared. It is important for the pastor to share the spotlight of the platform with many people. Prayer, Scripture reading, and announcements can all be done by Christians in the church. People can be taught through personal instruction and books how to read aloud and be concise in speaking (see Letter 2 in Appendix). Midweek Bible studies can be led by the men of the church when they realize that this function isn't necessarily "what we hired the pastor to do."

After searching the Scriptures we discovered that any Christian can scripturally baptize another. The pastor at Temple baptizes less than half the converts each year. Fathers almost always baptize their own children. That is so much more meaningful to the child, the family, and the whole church. Our campus worker baptizes all his converts. Husbands baptize their wives. And, I suppose, we'll one day have to face the question of whether or not a wife can baptize her husband. This concept is much more biblical than the tradition of the pastor doing all the baptizing. No one who seriously studies Acts 2 believes that the twelve apostles baptized 2,000 people in one day. That would have been physically impossible. Those Christians were examining and baptizing each other.

Another tradition that has disappeared at Temple in order to share the ministry is the presence of the pastor during the serving of communion. The men of the church explain who is invited to the Lord's Supper and what it means according to our understanding of the Bible. The men serve the elements, lead the entire service, and direct people when to partake. It's really beautiful. The ministry is shared.

Sharing the ministry means that more people will accept responsibility because they understand that true authority will be given with responsibility. The pastor is no longer the bottleneck through which all details must pass. The Music Committee meets without the pastor and sets up the special music, accompanists, and choir programs. The trustees care for the buildings and grounds. The Christian Education Board functions whether the pastor is present or not. Sometimes the pastor must teach this concept by *refusing* to do some of the detail work around the church. It's easy for a committee to dump the "legwork" onto the pastor: "After all, he has time to make the phone calls, send the letters, and pick up the materials downtown." Oh, no, he doesn't! Sharing the ministry works both ways. The people responsible for each area must do their own legwork. The pastor isn't an "errand boy." Neither are the people of the church.

Findley Edge attacks a fear of some about the shared ministry:

> *"What we need to understand at this point is that this is not a devious plan which a group of scheming preachers worked up to try to trap the laity into doing work that preachers don't want to do. Neither is it a malicious program planned in some denominational head-quarters to tap a vast untapped resource of manpower. This is God's design for the accomplishing of his re-demptive mission in the world, and we have missed it! It is God's plan and we have been trying some other way. Regardless of what our theology may be theoretically, in actual fact and practice we have been relying upon the wrong people as ministers for God"* (The Greening of the Church, p. 40).

## 5. WILLINGNESS TO CHANGE

Churches must be willing to change. In a day of high mobility and rapid change, many churches still operate as they did forty years ago in rural America. They complain about mobility rather than use it for the glory of God. "We lost four key families last month," a preacher laments. "Just as we get people into places of leadership, they move." "We train them, but we can never use them before they move." Such statements are true of every church, especially those near military installations, campuses, and businesses depending on government contracts.

Rather than dwelling on the obvious disadvantages of mobility, churches should search for blessings in mobility.

One Sunday as I stood to preach I noticed that on the front row our choir director was crying. After the service I asked her if I could help. "No," she sighed, "I'm just feeling sorry for myself. Several of our best choir members informed me today that they're either leaving the area or have to change to the other morning service and leave the choir." Yet Sally herself is a military wife. She and her family leave a church every three or four years. They are active Christians (her husband is a deacon), so when they go they really leave a hole. Now Sally was seeing the problem in a new light. It was good for her. And it gave me an opportunity to show her the good things about people's leaving.

One positive factor in people's leaving is that they will help spread the ministry. Since we minister to many military families we rejoice that a "little piece of Temple" is spread wherever our people move. They take our church's love, enthusiasm, and concept of ministry to their new church. We warn them not to begin life there with excessive chatter about their last church. But they are encouraged to spread their knowledge tactfully.

Mobility also helps us to understand more vividly the New Testament's teaching of the unity of the Body. We know that wherever our people move, they will almost certainly find true Christians who are growing in Christ. Moving frequently helps

Christians to minister in many different situations. It helps them reach a greater number of people for evangelism.

Part of the church's responsibility is to help people who move frequently learn to cope with that lifestyle. People on the move are tempted not to enter into deep personal relationships with others, because the relationships will be broken when the inevitable transfer comes. Stable people in the community may avoid getting emotionally attached to transient families. But Christians should be urged to make commitments to each other, even though they may be short-lived. Those who move often should learn to enjoy every minute of their lives and ministries in their present environment. They should "settle in" quickly, put up curtains, join the local church, take places of responsibility. After all, God is in control. Maybe this is their last move.

If a transient family has children who are already away from home (college, marriage, military), the church has additional responsibilities. The children may visit their parents less frequently than usual, since the new town won't be "home" to them. They will feel strange in church. Their friends won't be there. So the church should make a special effort to include these children at vacation times and holidays when they come to see their parents.

Willingness to change also means ability to ditch the past. Often churches keep a tight grip on programs, institutions, and committees that actually died years ago. When a program is no longer useful, it should be buried. When committees are no longer needed, they should be dissolved. An idea that doesn't work should be dropped. In our situation the traditional Sunday evening youth group approach didn't work. So we quit trying and changed the format. Our men's fellowship meetings were groaning with pain. We buried the whole organization and danced on its grave.

At one point we were within two weeks of not having an adult choir. Then it was revitalized and kept. Several committees have died, and a couple of organizations now have terminal illnesses. The idea is that any program, time, place, committee, or group that gets in the way of *meaningful* ministry must yield.

At the same time new programs must be born to meet new and changing needs. The last seven words of the church, "We never did it that way before," should never be heard among Christians who want renewal. It doesn't matter if no one else has done it before. Try it anyway. If it doesn't meet your needs in your church, change or drop the idea. Almost all new programs and ideas should be thought of as temporary. They last as long as they work. As long as the vehicle fits into the limitations of Scripture, it should be used.

We had never heard of any church taking primaries (grades 1-3) on overnight camp outs. (This isn't to say no one ever did. We just didn't know of any.) So we tried it. It worked. It was spiritually profitable. So now we do it every summer. The same is true for weekday field trips for children. Our elders' Family to Family program links a new family with an established family in the church (see Letter 3 in Appendix). This program and our Sunday school elective program are probably similar to what others have done. But our ventures were custom-made for our situation. We copy ideas, sometimes, but we tailor-make the program to fit *us*.

Renewal is often hindered when people refuse to evaluate *every* part of the church. Each nut and bolt must be scrutinized in light of the question, "Why are we doing this?" Singing the doxology, repeating the Apostles' Creed, sitting in pews, using a prayer book or hymnal, wearing (or not wearing) ministerial robes, giving to missions, contributing to the denomination, the pastoral prayer, kneeling for prayer, altar calls, and organ music *must* be evaluated periodically. A few things may be really sacred in your setting, but you should go after the rest with a critical eye. In our nonliturgical tradition, only the Bible and ordinances are sacred. Everything else is carefully evaluated and must meet tough standards or be dismissed.

People enjoy fresh approaches. First-person sermons are especially beneficial for holidays. An Easter sermon can be brought to life by assuming the role of Cleopas and telling the story of Luke 24 in the first person. Question-and-answer sermons or question periods after sermons help people enter into the message. Simply changing the order of services every two months is a relief. Placing soloists offstage and out of view helps people concentrate on the words. Choirs and speakers entering from different parts of the auditorium capture attention early in the service. Making announcements offstage with a microphone keeps the congregation awake during a usually boring time in the service. During communion, pictures flashed on a screen, or a solo can be inspiring. Receiving an offering from the back row first (or vice versa if you are locked into that tradition) helps call special attention to that form of worship.

Change is not sacred by itself. Creativity for the sake of being clever is not valid. But fresh approaches to old concepts would be more acceptable than most church leaders realize.

## 6. RESPONSIBLE LEADERSHIP

Leaders of a church should be recognized, not chosen. This is important. The ministry can't be shared and changes can't be instituted quickly unless those in places of responsibility are responsible Christians. Paul and Barnabas were chosen by the Holy Spirit and recognized by the church for missionary duty (Acts 13:1-3).

That is not the way most churches choose leaders. The Christian Education Committee or Personnel Committee or Nominating Committee gathers and tries to find names to "fill the slots." Anyone who is regular in attendance, not involved in any overt sin that any committee member knows about, and will take the job—can have it. Usually no training is offered, no job description is written, no challenge is issued. The available one is simply told that "the Lord led" the committee to ask him to take the job. If he doesn't take it, no one else will. Besides, not much commitment is involved. "Here is the manual produced by the denomination. Just read this and all your questions will be answered."

The alternative to the above chaos is the time-consuming method of developing leaders. At Temple we began by writing job descriptions for every position in the church, using this format: name of the position, person to whom responsible, general responsibilities, specific responsibilities, qualifications, authority, and relationships. When we have an opening for a leadership position we spend time praying for God's person for that position. If no one seems to appear we must consider the possibility that God wants the position abolished.

Leaders are not developed simply by giving people places of responsibility. Leaders must first prove themselves faithful in small things around the church. We reject the idea that we should "give Harry a place to serve to help him be more faithful." Frankly, we have lost many potential members by taking this hard line. When "Mr. Christian" moves to town he often visits several churches of his stripe before he settles down. In each church he humbly tries to impress the leaders with his past record of Christian involvement. What he hopes will happen usually does: he is offered immediate opportunities to serve the Lord in that particular church. But our church doesn't offer him a position immediately. Rather, he is informed that he is welcome to enter the Body at Temple and become part of the group. He will need time to understand the concept of ministry here. He is asked just to sit and learn and be ministered to, before he tries to minister. Then as he shows himself faithful and mature, certainly he will be able to minister in the Body.

Leaders are most frequently developed by one person's investing time in another. Each elder is encouraged to reproduce himself in another person so that we have a constant flow of elders into that program. We set up a system of assistants in most jobs so that one person is always training another. One concept we try to impart to each potential leader is the importance of being responsible. If a leader drops the ball, we all suffer the consequences. In our system leaders have opportunities to carry the ball by themselves with their own group. So they must be prepared to follow through with their responsibilities.

## 7. A CARING COMMUNITY

At Temple Baptist Church, God has given a willingness to cooperate with other Christians. Temple's buildings are used more than seventy-seven hours per week. We are delighted that God's people in Colorado Springs know the church as a place with a cooperative, not exclusive, spirit. The church allows its buildings to be used for a Christian day school. Christian groups such as the Navigators frequently use the buildings. One complex of offices is donated to Colorado Springs Right To Life (a pro-life, secular organization), a Christian bookstore, and a Christian counseling organization.

The church makes an honest attempt to minister to the community. The idea is not to get warm bodies in the church buildings, but as Findley Edge says,

> *"It is to the world to which we are called. We are not sent to serve the church but to the world as an instrument of redemption. Thus we are not called to attend meetings in the institutional church merely to keep certain organizations alive and growing. It is the world we are seeking to save, not the institution. The church is to lose its life and as it does so, it will find that it has fulfilled its calling"* (The Greening of the Church, p. 169).

Several summers ago we noticed that in a nearby community, no church was reaching the large summer transient population of young people. We rented a building in that community, hired a director, and opened a coffeehouse. We trained our own people to work with these hard-core, counter-culture youth. Most of us didn't appreciate the music or the decor of the coffeehouse. But over 100 young people gave their lives to Christ that summer. Our people not only invested their money and prayers, but frequently were asked to open their homes on short notice for "crashers." A few of these overnight guests "ripped off" some things and at least once we later discovered we had been harboring a wanted criminal. Middle-class Christians served as gracious hosts to those who were altogether in a different culture. When these counterculture people would attend church in their native garb, no one batted an eyelash. Jeans, headbands, sandals, and bare feet are well accepted in our worship services.

One of the best outreaches of the coffeehouse that first summer was an offer of free peanut-butter or tuna sandwiches. We made the sandwiches and gave them away without any charge at 4-6 P.M. each day before the coffeehouse opened and the bands started playing. The sign read, "These sandwiches are supplied by some Christians who love you." More than a few "freaks" said that those words almost "blew their minds," especially when they discovered that the Christians were in a church—and a Baptist church at that! That outreach meant long hours, late nights, and situations most of us had never encountered. What do you do, for instance, when a young man and woman you let crash for the night have been traveling across the country for three weeks sleeping together, although they aren't married? Do you let them sleep together in your home? Because he lights up a "joint," do you remove a young man from the coffeehouse who is interested in talking about Jesus' claim on his life? That summer ministry convinced the church of the need to reach young people in the community. Since then we have bought a house, extensively remodeled it, and now have a year-round coffeehouse ministry. Some of those early converts are now solid Christians in the Body.

The church also sponsors a campus worker on a nearby college campus. There is no pressure on the worker to "bring them in," meaning into our particular church. The worker uses our coffeehouse for meetings and counseling. The present coffeehouse, like the first one, does not advertise for the church in any way. Our name never appears in, on, or around the building. The college students are not being "hustled" for Temple.

Each week we send out fifteen to twenty letters of comfort to families who have recently lost loved ones in death (see Letter 4 in Appendix). The letter is strictly comfort. It doesn't even suggest that they visit our church. Every week, "thank you" notes are received in response to this ministry. We are always open to hospital visitation of people who have no church home. We view our mission as sharing Christ and helping others, regardless of whether or not they will become Christians, and certainly whether or not they will ever attend our church.

# 3

*Opposition*

Dear friends, don't be bewildered or surprised when you go through the fiery trials ahead, for this is no strange, unusual thing that is going to happen to you. . . . Be happy if you are cursed and insulted for being a Christian.

1 Peter 4:12, 14 [TLB]

Christians are told in the New Testament to expect some opposition. Jesus warned his followers that the world will oppose Christians, "and these things will they do unto you, because they have not known the Father, nor me" (John 16:3).

Temple has faced opposition, gone to battle, and (for a time) seemed to lose. Since the battle, however, God's plan has been seen more clearly, and we realize that our "loss" was for God's glory and our gain.

As the church began to expand rapidly, the leaders recognized a need for expanded facilities. A church should never emphasize facilities before people or ministry. But people do need a place to sit that is warm and dry. Several alternatives were considered. The governing board of the church spent hours reaching their own conclusions about the philosophy of the ministry.

One alternative was to begin another church in our city. After long and prayerful searching, that alternative was dismissed, at least for the time. Although we are the only church of our denomination in Colorado Springs, many of the newer churches have a similar concept. Several solid Bible-teaching, gospel-preaching witnesses have been born in the last few years. None of these churches has exactly our emphasis, but some are pretty close. We reject the idea that many small churches can do a better job than fewer, larger churches. Small churches (less than 200 attendance) spend a great deal of time and effort just struggling for existence. The monthly budget, the need for adequate facilities, too few people doing too much work are constant problems. The loss of one or two families can cripple a small church. The small church rarely has a dynamic impact on its society for Christ. Smaller churches are often unstable because pastors come and leave more frequently.

Undoubtedly larger churches tend to lose some closeness and friendliness that smaller churches enjoy. But small groups within the church can meet fellowship needs very nicely when they are structured to solve that problem. Smaller churches tend to rely more heavily on the pastor for all the work of the ministry. A larger testimony tends to spread the ministry among its members, simply because more members are available to help. Naturally the large church has more "pew warmers," since they can remain somewhat anonymous in a large crowd. The "sitters" who come sit in the larger church at least hear the Word, even if they don't put it into use right away.

Another problem with starting another church is trying to decide who goes and who stays. The established work offers better facilities and Christian training for one's family. One who may be willing to sacrifice some luxuries himself prays twice before sacrificing the needs of his children. They grow up only once. People who chose a church primarily because of the preacher and his message may resist having to uproot and sit under a different preacher. One way to start a new work is simply to tell those members who live in a certain geographic location that they're expected to attend the young church. One church in our city tried that and failed. People didn't like to be told which church to attend. Protestants rebel at that kind of authoritarianism. That church dropped its second morning service when the new work started. In one month they were back to two services, not because of growth, but because people "assigned" to the new church came dribbling back. And in this case the new work had taken the senior pastor.

Our conclusion was, therefore, not to start another church at that time. We considered purchasing houses near the church and using them for educational space, eventually removing them to build buildings. However, this would be a very expensive route to purchase land. The price of one lot with a house on it, which would eventually be removed, would be about the same as for several acres of land elsewhere.

So, we decided to relocate the entire church plant. We had our facilities appraised and put the church on the market. Then we started looking for suitable land. We looked and looked. I felt like a real estate agent myself after several months of looking at available land.

Finally we found nineteen and a half wooded acres near the interstate highway. That seemed to be what we needed. Our chief requirement was access. Already we had agreed that we were not a neighborhood church. We don't try to be. We never will be. Nowadays, people don't necessarily expect to live close to their employment or to shopping centers. There are few "neighborhood schools." In fact, there may be few neighborhoods, in the traditional sense. So we live with the fact that we are a commuting church. Very few people walk to church. Everyone drives. We needed to be near a major thoroughfare. Some of our people drive to Temple from the nearby mountains twenty miles away. Some commute weekly from Denver, sixty miles one way. They drive from every direction, so it didn't really matter in which end of town the church was located. This particular piece of land was in the northern section of the city.

The price was right, so the church put $5,000 earnest money on the property, signing a contract with several options. We started studying the situation. We hired an architect. Research into the project was intense. A planner was retained. He wanted to purchase part of the property from us as payment for his engineering and planning work. We agreed. Everything was sailing along smoothly until we discovered that some of the homeowners in the area objected to our presence. Homes in the area sold for $50,000 and up. Covenants and restrictions on the neighborhood made it a very exclusive part of the city.

We asked for a meeting with the homeowners' organization. We volunteered to give them several acres they thought desirable as a "greenbelt" area. We promised to design the church to fit in with the neighborhood's shake shingles and natural rock. We assured them that the new gym and playground would be available for community use. We wanted to be good neighbors and serve the area. But nothing helped. Some of those people just didn't want a church in their neighborhood. They objected to the traffic it would bring, although only about one percent of the traffic would go through residential streets. They objected to the "noise." They objected to the parking lot which would be part of the complex. So we agreed to meet them before the City Planning Commission.

Our first encounter before the city was confused. The homeowners dwelt on their right to the greenbelt area. We countered that we had already offered to give that area free of charge to the homeowners. The Planning Commission tabled our request for approval and sent us back to the homeowners to work out a detailed plan for the greenbelt. Again we met with the group. Again they balked. This time we threatened to tell the city that they weren't cooperating with the greenbelt plan simply because they didn't want a church in their neighborhood. We agreed on terms.

The second encounter before the city was ugly. The homeowners' association had spread several half-truths about the church. They had written the city council members. We had decided that our weapon was prayer, not pressure. We wrote no letters, and did not attempt to circulate any petitions. Homeowners turned out en masse to protest the building of the church. The Planning Commission zoned the land with a zone which required that a detailed master plan be submitted for public debate. Every time any structure was planned for the property we would be open for public debate. The homeowners openly declared that they would oppose *any* plans to build.

So, we won, but we lost. We had permission to build, but we would be hassled at every move. I told the Planning Commission in the debate that we would not appreciate this type of zoning. We felt that we must obey the city because we were Christians. We were scripturally subject to their authority. But we felt no obligation to be in subjection to surrounding homeowners. We would not let them tell us how to build our church. After prayer and discussion the church assigned its option to the engineer and planner who had helped us. We had spent six months, still had no land, and were more crowded than ever.

Knowing that God is in control, we thanked him for the experience and started looking again. This time we looked right next door. A two-story medical and dental building sat next to the church. It had a full basement, elevator, air conditioning, and was well constructed. Once before the owner had tried to sell us the building. We had decided then that (1) it wouldn't meet our needs for more auditorium space, (2) it was chopped into small examining rooms that wouldn't be suitable for educational space, and (3) the price was too high. But now we agreed to reconsider the building. The price had been reduced by $40,000. The building could be remodeled for educational space. But it definitely would not help our need for auditorium space. After several months of investigation and research we did purchase the building for $60,000 less than the original price quoted to us and $132,000 less than the seven-year-old building originally cost. God had shown us his will.

Extensive remodeling began on the second floor of the new building. The Building Committee took complete charge. I pulled back from involvement. Wise contract negotiating and thrifty purchasing allowed us to remodel and carpet the building for $7,000. All estimates had run from $15,000 to $20,000. At the same time two walls were removed from our old auditorium, and a more extensive children's church was put into operation. We were already having double services. Now we could accommodate the growth in the auditorium. Opposition had turned to blessing. The immediate "crisis" for space was over. Already we are searching for land again since our projections show that we will outgrow all the present facilities in three years.

Opposition from the world really didn't bother us. We took it as evidence that we were going in the right direction. The next rock of opposition, however, caught me completely off guard.

Several ministers in our area decided that it would be profitable to have an interchurch meeting on a Sunday night after our regular services. My assistant pastor and I attended the planning meeting. It started late and I had to leave for another appointment before it was over. After I left, the group decided to have each minister take a part of the service. They wanted me to have some of the liturgy. My assistant explained that I didn't know much about liturgy, but that I would probably be available to read Scripture. I agreed.

Temple was never an official part of the service. We didn't advertise the meeting in our church paper or bulletin. Our assistant pastor had persuaded the ministers to have an evangelical layman from a Presbyterian church as speaker (none of the others was Presbyterian). On the day of the service I announced that the interchurch service would be held. My announcement was that "You are invited. An evangelical is speaking." At the service, I left after reading Scripture.

Looking back upon the incident, I have ambivalent feelings. I'm glad I participated, so that the other ministers know we don't fit their image of a withdrawn, exclusive evangelical. But the service was poorly attended, not at all spiritually profitable, and essentially a waste of time.

The problem came when an article in the local newspaper linked my name and Temple with the service. A pastor in Denver somehow got hold of the article, misquoted part of it, and used it to blast the denomination of which I am a part. Having left our denomination some years before, he used the article to show the "degeneration" of those who remain in the group. The concluding statement of this brother's article was: "We need men who will stand true to the Word of God!"

That crushed me. I expected opposition from the world, the flesh, and the devil, but not from a fellow pastor. I had never been personally attacked like that before. My few years in the pastorate, and my youth (I was born the year we entered World War II) did not prepare me for such tactics. I felt I was giving my life to stand true to the Word of God. Yet this man, who didn't know me or the church I pastored, was hacking away at my testimony as a Christian and as a minister. I was really depressed.

My first action came only minutes after I read his article. I prayed for the author. I prayed that God would bless him and use him. I had to do that. If I hadn't done that right away, the bitterness that was knocking at my heart would have come in and swamped me. I was tempted to pray for God's judgment on the man, but God's grace protected me from trying to call down fire from heaven on others.

In the following days I wrestled with what to do. Frankly, I considered everything from kindly explaining the facts to the man, to punching him in the nose, to doing nothing. I chose the latter. My assistant, who knew the pastor well, convinced me that he was not likely to admit an error or to accept my explanation. So I did nothing, and instructed my assistant to do nothing. A few weeks later a fellow pastor from Denver told me that he had read the article, knew it must be slanted and in error, and asked me for the facts. He had already tried to defend me to the man who wrote the article, but said he needed more information. I said, "Dave, I appreciate your concern, but please don't defend me. The matter is dropped."

At least, I thought the matter was dropped. Several weeks later two pastors in California picked up the story from my critic's church newspaper, and printed it in their church papers with a few added "facts" of their own. One article criticized not only my denomination but also my home church, seminary, and wife for being involved with me.

Opposition opens the door to God's love. How difficult it would be to love our detractors without the supernatural power to love and "pray for those who despitefully use you." Opposition provides a clear choice between bitterness and love. Opposition must certainly be one of those "fiery trials" Peter talks about and the "various trials" James mentions.

The concept of sharing the ministry is very threatening to some professional ministers. At a retreat for ministers and their wives, the group divided up to discuss discipleship and what each was doing to disciple others. I had already decided not to say anything. I kept my mouth closed, listened to others, and was generally enjoying learning. Then a fellow pastor asked me to share what was happening at Temple in the area of discipleship. I choked up. My throat went dry, and I started to tremble. But remember, I address groups large and small several times a week. So this wasn't "stage fright." It was fear of my brothers in Christ.

After I stammered out a few words about sharing the ministry, one pastor growled, "Yes, but you have a higher caliber of Christians than the rest of us." I wanted to tell him about our church's history of fighting and splitting. I was tempted to take thirty minutes to explain that mature Christians don't "happen"; you have to develop them. But I didn't. I'm young and have a lot to learn, and I don't know about other churches. So I just answered, "Maybe so. I don't know." By this time another minister chimed in, expressing his displeasure at a minister who doesn't control the midweek service, baptism, and the Lord's Supper. He asked if I was training someone to take over the preaching on Sunday morning. I answered that I wasn't. "Well," he quipped, "get someone to do that, and you won't have anything to do."

That kind of opposition stings. I am always disappointed when Christians fail to give other Christians latitude to do the work of the ministry in the way that seems most scriptural to them. I find it depressing even to recall these events.

# 4

## Pastor's Prayer Corps

**For the Lord is watching his children, listening to their prayers.**

1 Peter 3:12 [TLB]

When I assumed the pastorate of Temple, I realized that my new ministry would include a group with whom I had had little contact: the "Geritol generation." The Lord almost immediately impressed me with the needs of the senior citizens of the congregation. My usual emphasis was young people, so I had to be careful not to neglect those who were elderly.

During my first week I began visiting each elderly person of the congregation. One afternoon I called on 332 years of people in only four visits! As I talked with these saints, their needs poured from their hearts. They needed to be needed. They often felt worthless to God and man. I frequently found that I was good-naturedly scolding some of my new friends when they would sigh, "I'm so old, all I can do is pray." On each occasion I would reply, "*All* you can do is pray? What do you mean by that?" Then I would point out the importance of prayer.

After visiting these folks for two weeks, the Lord spoke to me about this untapped resource of prayer power. These elderly people have a ministry and a spiritual gift of prayer. They have time to pray, and they enjoy praying. Yet, no one was helping them develop their gift and ministry. As a pastor, that is my calling. So I went to work.

First, I typed a letter to each one, an invitation to join the "Pastor's Prayer Corps":

*Dear* _____ :
　　*Since our visit together last week the Lord has been*

*speaking to me concerning your gift and ministry of prayer. Because the Lord has given you this gift and the time to use it, I think my responsibility is to help you. For this reason I am forming "PASTOR'S PRAYER CORPS."*

*I would like for you to be part of my personal prayer corps. Each week I will send you a list of requests for you to pray for. Some of the requests will be personal, others will be for the church, and others will be for individuals who have asked me to pray for specific things and have given me permission to ask the Prayer Corps to help.*

*"Pastor's Prayer Corps" will have no meetings or election of officers. Our communication will be through the weekly letter of requests. As God answers, I will include those answers in the weekly letter also.*

*If you would like to be part of "Pastor's Prayer Corps," then sign the enclosed card and mail it to me.*

*This week's prayer list is enclosed if you decide to help.*

*Sincerely in Jesus,*

I didn't know what kind of response to expect. Tuesday, the day after I mailed the letters, I mentioned the idea to an Air Force chaplain who is a member of our church. He predicted that all the cards would be returned by Friday. They were all in by Thursday.

One lady who hadn't been able to attend church for five years was in a pew the next Sunday. She has missed only one Sunday since, because of a snow storm. Every one of the Prayer Corps members testifies to the joy of receiving the letter each week. Each one faithfully prays for the requests. One lady who is ninety-two years old told me that she wakes up with the week's list on her mind each morning. In casual conversation, these elderly people easily recall the whole list of requests for that week.

Each Monday I type the letters with the requests and send them to the Prayer Corps. We have never had a week without answers to some of the requests.

The Prayer Corps is a quiet band of believers. We have never made any announcements about the plan. Most members of the church have never heard of it. Yet, I firmly believe that the source of power for our church is our Prayer Corps, composed of people who "can't do anything but pray."

At times I am tempted to enlarge the Prayer Corps but I don't for fear that some would join to "get in on the news" or just to please the pastor. Instead, we keep the group small, a hand-picked few who feel that their time remaining on this earth is to be spent in prayer. From time to time someone learns about the Prayer Corps and asks to join. I carefully explain that the purpose of the group requires a commitment of daily prayer for each of the requests. I suggest to the person that he consider it prayerfully for a few days. Then I send a follow-up letter with a self-addressed card asking for a final decision.

Often ideas splash upon my mind long before they become an even-flowing stream. While ideas are in the "splash" stage, I ask the Prayer Corps to pray with me about the thought. Sometimes the idea develops, sometimes it dies. But prayer makes me assured of God's will in most instances. On one or two occasions I've called my friends on the carpet and gently rebuked them. You see, I *know* when the Prayer Corp is praying. On a few occasions when my week has been frustrated, awkward, and ineffective, I've checked my own life and prayer time with God. If things honestly seem to be in order, I lay the blame for a bad week at the feet of my prayer warriors. It has happened only a few times but I've turned out to be right each time. The next week is always a super week as those faithful Christians get back to the hard job of prayer on my behalf.

Our assistant pastor talks about "common, everyday miracles" at Temple. He is right. The reason for that is prayer power. The Pastor's Prayer Corps is quietly setting the example.

# 5

*Singles*

**Use hospitality one to another without grudging.**

1 Peter 4:9

SINGLES

Two of Temple's faithful members were sisters, Ruth and Jane. They are in their mid-and late twenties. Ruth is a school teacher and the church organist. Jane is a nurse. Both are quiet, nice looking, talented, committed Christians, and single. There was always a place in the church for these two to minister, but never a place where they really *fit*. They could attend the college class where they were older than the others and certainly more mature. Or, they could attend the young marrieds class where the members were their own age, but surely had different interests. The solution was that Ruth always taught a children's class, and Jane worked on Sunday mornings at the hospital and taught a weekday girls' group. No one liked the solution. These two women are well-respected and loved by Temple, but they are *single*. And in spite of 1 Corinthians seven many churches still treat single people as second-class Christians. They don't mean to, they just don't plan *not* to.

Primarily because of Ruth and Jane we decided to try a class for singles. We had no visions of what God was going to do. One year after I met with the first few singles the class was *averaging* 75 people a week! It is one of the most enthusiastic, vibrant, exciting, and growing ministries in the church.

Several principles help the ministry to grow. First, we emphasized the need of God's Word for each life. Single people in today's society have some heavy pressures to conform to the ways of the world. Drugs, drinking, and sexual looseness are part of the life of many singles without Christ. The need for acceptance and love from peers is strong in the single's heart. So unless the church meets those needs through the Word the single Christian adult may soon crumble under his load and be lost as a servant of the Lord. The single adult has time and ability to dig deep in serious Bible study. His needs dictate that he be challenged to do that regularly and systematically.

The curriculum for the class varies as do our other adult electives. Sometimes they study a book of the Bible, verse-by-verse. At other times they have had topical studies or studied Christian books. We try to give the class a balanced diet for the Christian experience.

Second, we let the class run its own affairs. The group elects a committee of seven men and women to lead it. We have a deacon and his wife there simply to serve as ex-officio members and to be a liason to the Board of Deacons when that is necessary. I meet with the president of the group and challenge him to serve as a pastor over that group. After all, leading a group of 100 people (counting those who are in and out) is no small task. The group has its own weekday home Bible studies which are coordinated with Temple's other home Bible studies. The group has a job description for each committee member, and its stated purpose is "Spiritual Growth, gained from a study of the Word, expressed through fellowship, resulting in outreach."

The group consciously makes an effort not to be
a church in and of itself. Rather it is an organ of the
Body at Temple. They meet every week after the
evening service for fellowship. But when the church
has its once-per-month time of refreshments, they
decided to be a part of the total church fellowship
time instead.

The committee makes suggestions to the Christian Education Board of the church about its curriculum and teacher for the quarter. There has
never been any conflict because there is a spirit of
love and cooperation on all sides.

We are cautious, however, that the group not
lose its identity with Temple. The singles operate
their own affairs, but we work to maintain a close
connection with the church. It is possible for such a
group to drift into the sea of the world and lose its
distinctives. This could happen to such a group with
the pure motives of trying to reach their world for
Christ. But soon the group might sponsor activities
which do not fit into the total approach of the particular local church, and the entire singles ministry
would be jeopardized. We have seen this happen to
another local church in our city. Many who attend
that group never know it was started by and is still
sponsored by a church. There is nothing distinc-
tively Christian about the group other than the fact
that some of its leaders are Christians.

Third, we accept divorcees as people, not lepers.
Each church who wishes to have a singles ministry
*must* face this issue. Even if the church believes that

all divorce is wrong and all re-marriage is sin, that position doesn't mean that those divorced should be excluded from the Body-life and love of the church. No thinking Christian believes that God forgives all sin except divorce. The church must stop picking on those who made certain mistakes but have confessed those errors to God. Divorcees can be clean, whole, respectable Christians who love God and are growing in Christ! Don't overlook this great ministry to a large section of our society.

Christian divorcees want to know what the Bible says about divorce and re-marriage. The leaders of the church should dig into the Bible and come to some conclusions to help these people. Having a successful singles ministry does not necessarily mean that the church must take a soft line on divorce and re-marriage. We don't. It just means that the church must forgive and love and want to help divorcees, which is a reasonable request and position.

The fourth principle is that a singles ministry must provide many hours of fellowship. Singles will be with singles somewhere, so why shouldn't it be church. And it better be filled to the brim. For unless it is, the single adult will be tempted to the bar-hopping habits of his friends at work. Big crowds are drawn to the activities planned every week in addition to the Sunday activities. It is interesting to see how non-Christians are attracted to wholesome activities when couples are not pairing off in bedrooms and liquor does not flow. Part of the fellowship consists of several weekend retreats each year. There is a level of fellowship there that exists nowhere else during the year. One year we tried combining the singles' and married adults' retreats. They met at the same camp, ate together and enjoyed recreation together. It worked beautifully. We now plan to continue that approach, but have a different set of seminars and speakers for each group.

A singles' ministry could happen in almost any city church. Of course, one does have to beware of the fellow or girl who attends such a group just looking for a bed partner. But even those people can be won to Christ and incorporated into the Body. We have found single adults to be excellent teachers of children. Our children especially are attracted to single young men who teach them. We employ singles in choirs, as choir directors, and as musicians and singers. Singles occupy leadership positions on boards and committees. They contribute to every part of the Body.

When I see what God has done in giving Temple the largest singles ministry of any church in Colorado Springs in only one year, I tremble to think that this opportunity was almost by-passed because we weren't seriously looking for people in the community who really want help and are searching for a ministry.

# 6

## Habits of Holiness

Obey God because you are his children; don't slip back into your old ways—doing evil because you knew no better. But be holy now in everything you do, just as the Lord is holy, who invited you to be his child.

1 Peter 1:14, 15 [TLB]

Habit is either the best of servants or the worst of masters. Some habits annoy other people, like polluting the air with cigarette smoke, or repeatedly borrowing without returning. Mark Twain once wrote, "Nothing so needs reforming as other people's habits." Some habits undress your soul and reveal who you really are. Habits of selfishness and laziness do that. Other habits develop from carelessness, like eating too fast or too much. Reckless driving and nagging are habits that develop unconsciously.

Habits can work for good also. The habit of getting up at the same time each morning makes it easier to swing your feet over the side of the bed to touch the floor. The habit of good table manners means you won't be self-conscious about your manners at the company party. The importance of habits was known by the philosopher Publilius Syrus, who lived the generation before Jesus. He wrote, "Powerful indeed is the empire of habit." In our century William James wrote, "Habit is thus the enormous fly wheel of society, its most precious conservative agent. It alone is what keeps us all within the bounds of ordinance" (*The Principles of Psychology,* chapter ten). The Bible explains that Christians should have habits, too: holy habits. They are referred to by the term "sanctification."

Sanctification is practicing habits of holiness. At Temple we are learning that holy living pleases God and makes Satan angry. We feel that we should be involved in both projects. In John 17:17, Jesus prayed to his heavenly Father on behalf of his disciples, "Sanctify them through thy truth: thy word is truth."

Certain principles will help us understand this or any other doctrine of the Bible. First, any doctrine (the word simply means "teaching") must be rightly related to other teachings. For example, it is important to understand that sanctification follows regeneration. Sanctification should not be overemphasized or minimized, but taught in balance with all scriptural truth. I have discovered that when a Christian or a group of Christians overemphasizes a particular doctrine, they are almost always in error about it. I have seen examples of this with sanctification, spiritual gifts, the free will of man, the sovereignty of God, separation of Christians from the world, and use of the name "Jehovah."

Second, it is not valid to explain doctrine by experience. Doctrine must always explain experience. Abandonment of this principle by many Christians today is causing a flood of confusion in the church. Interpreting truth in the spotlight of experience rather than the warm objective rays from the Word results in unstable and shallow Christianity.

The third principle is to determine what the Bible says. It is not appropriate to respond, "But I was always taught . . ." or "I think . . ." or "But Dr. Bible Teacher says . . ." or "My denomination teaches . . . ." The question a Christian should ask about any doctrine is: "What does the Bible say?"

To help develop habits of holiness we seriously asked that question—what does the Bible say?—about sanctification. We discovered that the Bible speaks of four different kinds of sanctification. The word means "to set apart." The Bible uses the word to say that God is sanctified, that God sanctifies people, places, and things, and that man sanctifies God: he sets God apart in his thoughts (1 Peter 3:15). The word does not always mean "to make holy" and it does not always imply sinlessness or finality.

Note that 1 Peter 1:2 teaches *preliminary* sanctification: "Elect according to the foreknowledge of God the Father, through sanctification of the Spirit." Christians were set apart before the foundation of the world (Ephesians 1:4).

There is also *positional* sanctification. Paul wrote 1 Corinthians to some carnal Christians, yet he addressed them as "those who are sanctified" (1 Corinthians 1:2). He said they were set apart in the past with the continuing result that they are still set apart.

The third type of sanctification is found in Jesus' words in John 17:17. We might call it *progressive* sanctification since it grows by means of the Word of God. All of us surrender our lives to God in installments. We may not intend to do so, but we do. We may yield all we know to yield at a certain time. Our sincerity does not change the fact that there is more to learn and more to yield at another time. Even if we entirely live up to our present knowledge and light, tomorrow God may reveal more areas that need attention. Growing holy is a process.

The process of progressive sanctification is not always visible. A tree grows downward and upward at the same time. So does a Christian. Christian growth is not always a grin and a verbal public testimony. It can be pain and suffering. The rate of growth is not constant throughout our own life and may be faster or slower than the growth of others. This kind of sanctification is never complete in this life. It requires our cooperation with God's plan for our lives.

Sanctification involves being set apart *unto* God. Victory in the Christian life is won on our knees, not in the heat of battle. The victory is won on the *inside* of the Christian. The battle is to yield to God our spirit, attitude, heart. When that is done, the daily skirmishes with the world, the flesh, and the devil are won. Habits of holiness also must cause us to be separated *from* sin. Sensitivity to sin must increase. As our convictions increase in the area of details, our failures should decrease. In other words, we will become more sensitive to details of our lives that we once never considered sin. At the same time we should be winning spiritual victories so that our failures in the Christian life are fewer. It may be diagramed like this:

The dotted lines in the second diagram illustrate where we are at a given point in the Christian life, with convictions on the increase and failures on the decrease.

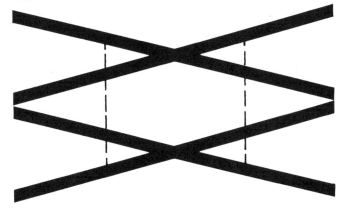

Habits of holiness help in the fight. Someone has written:

*Sow a Thought, and you reap an Act;*
*Sow an Act, and you reap a Habit;*
*Sow a Habit, and you reap a Character;*
*Sow a Character, and you reap a Destiny.*

Some habits we have attempted to create in Christians at Temple help to sow renewal. Christians are encouraged to make a habit of prayer. Regular, consistent, private prayer is constantly encouraged. Christians are urged to find a quiet place and pray in that same place every day. We also have group prayer at worship services, in the offices, and in classes. Special prayer-request sheets are distributed personally and through the mails. Christians are helped to make a habit of daily Bible study. We teach Bible study methods. We conduct small group studies for children, youth, men, women, and couples. Each year we enroll over 100 people in a simple "read through the Bible in a year" plan. Church attendance is a holy habit we try to create. We attempt to get Christians to settle the question once and for all, "Am I going to church this week?" Consistent Bible teaching, fellowship, and service help Christians grow more rapidly. Christians are shown how to develop the habit of sharing their faith in Christ. They are encouraged to witness "from the overflow of their lives." No one is cajoled to "witness to five people this week."

We're trying to destroy the image of Christians as spiritual schizophrenics. Some Christians have good doctrine but poor practice. They never let the Bible make contact with life, so their spiritual life is one big short circuit. Ministers sometimes reinforce this fragmentation with comments like, "I'm not going to preach doctrine this morning. I'm just going to be practical." Some Christians play the role of the super-duper saint with a mystical pseudo-spirituality. They hide behind pious assertions like, "I don't need anyone to teach me the Word. I'll just rely on the Holy Spirit." A favorite cliché, "The Lord led me," can be used to cover skipping church or transgressing any habit of holiness.

The fourth kind of sanctification taught in the Bible is *prospective* sanctification from 1 Thessalonians 5:23, "The God of peace sanctify you wholly." This occurs when progressive sanctification and positional sanctification become one, at the time when we see Jesus face to face.

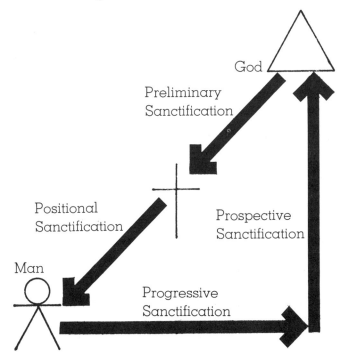

Every true Christian enjoys preliminary and positional sanctification. He was set apart for God before the foundation of the world was laid. He *is* set apart, so that God sees him not as a sinner, but as a holy one, through the cross. The true Christian will one day be caught up to be with the Lord, be given a new body, and enjoy complete sanctification. Our duty now is to make our daily lives as much like our position as possible: i.e., progressive sanctification.

Renewal demands holiness. Gimmicks, games, contests, and programs can never substitute for holy living in the church. Holy living among God's people may mean being more selective about those who lead the church. It will definitely demand concentrated effort and clean lives. Holy living is not to be confused with legalism or "list keeping." The Christian life brings freedom. Christians must not dictate to one another how holy living is to be defined. Each defines his own limits based upon his understanding of the Word and his place of spiritual maturity. But each of us *must* define. No one is exempt.

# 7
## More Staff

Are you called to preach? Then preach as though God himself were speaking through you. Are you called to help others? Do it with all the strength and energy that God supplies, so that God will be glorified through Jesus Christ—to him be glory and power forever and ever. Amen.

1 Peter 4:11 [TLB]

When God began renewal at Temple it became clear that another staff man was needed. We had already hired a part-time secretary. I had been at the church eight months when we began looking for a new staff person. The church wanted someone, not to do the work of the ministry, but to help me train people to enjoy their own ministry of reaching out to others. Nor did we want a "legman," someone to do what the pastor didn't want to do. We desired a qualified professional who could lead in the work.

Part of our problem was finding a full-time staff member who could work under the authority of a younger pastor. (I was 29 at the time.) We couldn't pay much, either. So, it seemed logical to us to scout for a recent seminary graduate. I traveled to a well-known school, interviewed scores of young men, and reported to the Deacon Board. We were well organized. We had created a beautiful, detailed three-page job description. Our goal was to try to find the man to fit our description. We knew what we wanted and we had put it down on paper.

After the first round of interviews we invited a young man to candidate for the position. He and his wife were flown to Colorado Springs, entertained, and interviewed. He was an extremely capable person and minister. In fact, the Board decided he was too capable. They realized that this graduate's gifts and abilities were such that he wouldn't long be happy in the position available. There was no discredit to the candidate or his gifts, in fact just the opposite. The Board recommended to the church that this fellow not be called. The church agreed.

I traveled to another seminary for a round of interviews, looking for the man to fill our slot. None did. We were discouraged. Then a member recommended a young man about to graduate from a seminary. He visited the church, was invited for an interview, and seemed to be our man. He fit our requirements, so we hired him.

In six months he was fired, and I landed in the hospital. We made a tragic mistake. We had forced people into program. We started at the wrong place and worked in the wrong direction. The new staff member couldn't keep up with the growth and pace of Temple. He was as inexperienced as most seminarians. The fault wasn't his, but ours. When I had worked on other church staffs, no senior pastor had ever had a regular meeting with me. I missed that, and decided to do things differently if I was ever the senior pastor of a church staff. So I met weekly with the new man. But I didn't do enough.

It was painful. I identified more with the staff member than with the people who began to complain about his ministry and lack of competence. I tried to protect him. I defended him, thinking it was terrible for a young man's first experience out of seminary to be a failure. I worked and prayed and talked—and failed. Finally, when no other option was open, he had to be dismissed. Through tears and prayers all but one couple in the church understood and agreed. The expense for me was a trip to the hospital for a week. Hospital tests showed that emotional pressure had created physical problems. That young man is now in another ministry and doing well for God's glory. We are friends, and occasionally see one another.

After such a devastating experience we were very slow to look for another person. This time our approach was entirely different.

Now, instead of

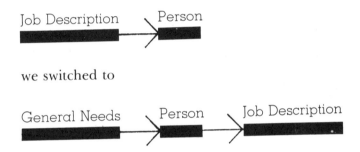

We are committed to this approach, realizing that in every other area we started with people and then moved to ministry. Somehow we had failed to follow our convictions in the area of hiring staff. We now see that God gives us a man, then we mold the job description to the man, not vice versa.

For five months we had no one else on the ministerial staff. Then God revealed that a member of the church was interested. Del Hafer hesitated to approach us because he didn't feel we would be interested in him. We had failed to approach Del because we didn't feel that he would be interested in the position. At the time he was director of Pikes

Peak Youth for Christ. He was several years older than I, and doing a terrific job with YFC. Having begun the local job when things were at their lowest point for YFC, Del had been used by God for "renewal" in that ministry. Their rallies, club work, personal work, and camp work were going great. Del had been with YFC for about fifteen years. He and his family were active members of Temple.

Del and I met often for snatches of fellowship. We communicated easily. Slowly we began to hint to each other that we might be interested in working together. We openly discussed the matter with one another, deciding that we should investigate the possibilities.

As a result, we have worked together very well since October 1972. Del is a deep man. He works from the original Hebrew and Greek in his presentations. He studies thoroughly. He outshines any of us in many areas of biblical knowledge. Del is dedicated to the ministry at Temple, and to me.

About the time Del joined the staff, Temple became the host church for Dave and Sally Fountain's work with Campus Ambassadors under the Conservative Baptist Home Mission Society. The Fountains were from California and had most recently been working at Northern Arizona University in Flagstaff. Temple helps support the Fountains, but they don't work directly for the church. They use our coffeehouse as a meeting place in their ministry. They funnel some students into Temple, but there is never pressure to do so. The mark of

Dave's success isn't the number of people in our college class on Sunday morning. God has used the Fountains to crack a tough campus for Christ. They work at a small, liberal college where students aren't hassled for sleeping together or smoking pot in the dorms. Several other Christian campus organizations had given up on this college before Dave and Sally came on the scene.

Seven months later our church needed another staff member. This man, too, was from within the Body. John Boaz had been a couple of years ahead of me at Dallas Theological Seminary. After his formal education, John and his wife, Charlotte, spent one year in an internship near Detroit and four years on the mission field in Japan, working under Far Eastern Gospel Crusade. The Boaz family moved to Colorado Springs for a year of furlough. When they first arrived we were hiring Del, and we couldn't afford another man at the time. The next summer, as John and his family were about to leave for Japan, devaluation of the American dollar hit. His return had to be postponed for a year. This put us back together to talk and pray about John's joining the staff. His children were already in the Christian school that meets in our buildings. He and his family had been active in the church.

Again we worked from general needs to the man to the specific job description. John joined the staff in September 1973, the same day we purchased the medical building.

Each summer we hire seminarians as summer interns. So far the interns have all been church members. In 1972, Dean Thomas from the Conservative Baptist Theological Seminary in Denver worked on our staff. Dean created the primary and junior field-trip and camp-out ministries. The next summer Doug Anderson from Dallas Seminary worked in the field-trip and camp-out and music ministries. Both of these men have done excellent jobs.

At present we are forming a counseling clinic to help people who hurt. In Acts 20:35, Paul admonished the Ephesian elders to "support the weak." The Greek word translated "weak" (*astheneo*) refers in other places to those who are physically sick (John 5:7), weak because of fear (2 Corinthians 11:21), religiously or morally weak (Romans 14:2), or economically weak (*A Greek-English Lexicon of the New Testament and other Early Christian Literature*, p. 115). The counseling ministry at Temple attempts to help all the "weak."

The need presented itself when all of the staff found ourselves with substantial counseling loads. Although the elders counsel their people, sometimes one who is hurting wants a "professional." But even a professional has only so many hours in the day. Once again God raised up people from within the Body. Several professional counselors moved into the community and began attending Temple. Some worked for the local mental health clinic or the military; others were school counselors. All were committed Christians. We met, discussed our approach to Christian counseling, and had a remarkable amount of agreement. We started on a part-time basis and with groups. Already this infant ministry is growing and we anticipate making a full-time director of counseling another staff position soon.

For the future we are also looking for a minister of discipleship. This person would teach disciple-makers. We want many Christians in the Body at Temple able to make disciples. Also we are looking for an executive minister, one who could coordinate the whole ministry at Temple. Additional staff members will help free me to study and preach the Word. In-depth preaching of the Word will keep Christians spiritually strong and help raise new Christians to maturity.

# 8

## How to Create Change

**Feed the flock of God; care for it willingly, not grudgingly; not for what you will get out of it, but because you are eager to serve the Lord.**

1 Peter 5:2 [TLB]

Church leaders, addressed as "elders" in 1 Peter 5:1, are given their marching orders in the next verse: Feed the flock of God. They are to serve willingly, not by constraint. I am so weary of pessimistic preachers who whine, "Nobody will work in my church. I'm not paid enough to make ends meet. So many of our good folks are leaving," and on and on. I propose that we ban these fellows from public meetings outside their own churches. If their own church is willing to live with their poor attitudes, that's okay. But let's not have such complainers loose on the rest of us. Pessimistic preachers who take a daily martyr's pill should stay in negative churches. They deserve each other!

Some churches don't want to change. Some pastors won't change. So let those two get together and "hold the fort." After I shared some of the material in this book at a conference, a young pastor came to me saying that he shared my ideas about the church. For three years he had been trying to bring the church he led to these ideas. But they refused to budge. They didn't want to change. They weren't interested in sharing the ministry. For the most part, no one cared if he had a spiritual gift or not. What they wanted was a comfortable pew, a respectable pastor, and a refuge from the world on Sunday. The young pastor was in his first church since seminary and asked me what he should do. My advice rocked him: *Leave.* That's right, leave the church. Go somewhere else. Look for a church that wants to change. Don't waste your life and ministry in a stagnant church that won't change after three years of loving leadership.

While lecturing at an evangelical seminary, I was frequently asked by students, "How do I influence the senior minister to accept these ideas if he is opposed to them when I join his staff?" My advice: Don't try to change him. A recent graduate on a church staff should either (1) live with the senior minister's concept of the ministry and fit into his approach, or (2) not work with him.

I do not counsel men to abandon local churches as pastor unless they have followed certain principles of change, and have given those principles a fair trial. Renewal and change are not mystical. I've told inquirers that I'm willing to share with them everything about the renewal of Temple. There are no gimmicks or magic buttons to push to create change. But there are some principles.

The first principle is to create change s-l-o-w-l-y. Two weeks after sharing some of Temple's changes at a pastor's retreat, I saw a young pastor who had been at the retreat. He greeted me with the news that he had taken most of our innovations and dumped them on his board—all at once. "Mike, they just looked at me and shook their heads as if to say, 'Don't ever try any of that foolishness around here.' " His church *is* trying to change. The problem was "too much too soon," and the men choked.

The second principle almost contradicts the first: Keep a challenge before the people you wish to change. Create change slowly, but keep at it. Many church leaders are bored with the simplistic way the church is operated. In our advanced space age we operate the church as we did years ago in rural America. We lack business management skills that would improve our efficiency. We fail to keep people awake because we lack vision to challenge them. On the same night we first considered purchasing the medical building next door (the price was then $220,000), I also had on the agenda a discussion of another staff member. I prefaced my remarks about the staff man with, "Gentlemen, I won't apologize for giving you so much to consider. We must press forward if we are to do the job God wants us to do."

Temple's governing board meets every week for business. We have that much business to consider. Our early morning meeting (6 A.M.) always lasts an hour and a half, sometimes two hours. Christians need to be challenged to think and plan, and pray *big*.

Another principle is: Be honest. Create change without manipulating people to your point of view. Be willing to be shot out of the saddle. Whenever I have a red-hot idea that needs attention, I begin to bounce it off different people of the church. I unload the idea and ask for honest evaluation. The people I communicate with in this manner know they have the freedom to be critical, brutally so if necessary. I appreciate that. I'm not trying to win them over to my way of thinking. I'm not trying to persuade them. I'm asking for evaluation.

By the time I bring my "world-changing plan" to

the board or committee involved, I have probably seen at least half of the group individually. I did not see them individually in order to "stack the committee" with my idea or manipulate people to vote for the new approach. But by the time I meet with the whole group I know most of their feelings and thoughts about the idea. I know their criticisms and I have been able to work on solutions. My idea has been burned and beaten and re-formed. If I still think it's valid, it has been refined enough to withstand the further evaluation of the whole committee. Usually the original idea has been enhanced by suggestions and deletions of the individuals I tried it out on prior to the committee meeting. Once again, however, I must realize that the idea may still be wrong at this time, for this situation, or in this place. I can't go to the committee with the thought of winning them over to my side. God leads through people on committees and boards too, not just through a few leaders.

Many times I've been glad that I didn't bully a group to follow my suggestions. There is a wall in our new educational building that I opposed. I thought building that wall was unnecessary and too expensive. But the Building Committee disagreed and built it anyway. They were right. I was wrong. Without that wall we would lose the efficiency of three classrooms.

For my first two years at Temple I wanted a constitutional change that would allow a deacon to serve a second three-year term without staying off the Board for a year. Each year Bill disagreed. Bill is older than I, and a wise, mature Christian. Each year we honestly faced each other and understood the other's reasons for his position. There was no compromise either of us could make. Each year I yielded. The third year I started off my presentation to Bill by saying that the formation of elders brought new data into the discussion. Some men who would be good deacons were elders and therefore not available to serve as deacons. We needed our deacons to be able to stay for another term. Bill agreed because of the new data. I was not trying to manipulate Bill or anyone else to get my way. I was trying to determine God's will for Temple about the matter. For two years it was God's will to leave the constitution as it had been. In 1973 the change was made. That was God's will, too.

In 1 Peter 5:2, church leaders are challenged to do their work "with a ready mind." I interpret that to mean that God's work is to be accomplished creatively. The flock can be fed in different ways. Although the diet must be from the Word, methods of feeding vary. Every part of a church's program must be evaluated. Why do we sit in pews, sing the doxology, receive an offering, repeat the Apostles' Creed? Is there a better way to do the same thing? Is an altar call (or lack of one) really the best method to help people respond to God's Word?

Having a "ready mind" to think creatively takes time. It is important for church leaders to have "think time." A pastor needs time to put his feet up on his desk to think through each part of the worship service. Each Christian leader in the church needs to consider, "How can I do it better? How can it be more interesting?" When the primary superintendent and the women's missionary leader and the adult Sunday school teacher begin thinking creatively along these lines, the church is on its way to change.

Church leaders blocked in their desire for change should recognize that they have not been appointed lords over God's dice (1 Peter 5:3). The Greek word translated "heritage" *(klar̄on)* is the word for *dice* or *lots.* In the Old Testament, God's people often discovered God's will by casting the lot. The idea was that God is in control of even the numbers which appear face up on dice. The thought in 1 Peter 5:3 is that each member of the group over which a leader has responsibility is there by divine appointment—even the cantankerous ones. The leader's job is not to bully the one who opposes him, but to be an example to him.

Sometimes people resist change because they lack confidence in the one desiring the change. Someone controlling a committee may oppose a person he doesn't appreciate as well as that person's idea when it comes before his committee. A Christian leader must be a godly example. When people view a life that pleases God, they are more likely to cooperate with the changes that person wants.

It is also my conviction that churches should organize and expect to change. Just as Dr. Donald

McGavran (Dean Emeritus of The School of World Mission and Institute of Church Growth at Fuller Theological Seminary, Pasadena, California) urges the church to expect growth, we must *expect* to change and *plan* to change. Every church leader should read *Self Renewal* (Harper and Row Publishers, 95¢, paper) by John Gardner. Replace the word "society" with the word "church" and you will have helpful insights on the methods of change. All of Temple's elders have been required to read and evaluate the 157 pages of that book. Gardner says, "It is not enough for a society (church) to recognize the need for renewal. It must have the institutional arrangements that make orderly change a possibility" (p. 83, parenthesis mine).

Too often however the church is not organized for renewal. It is organized for stagnation. Our thinking must be toward renewal. We must approach all parts of the church with the thought of renewal. That means we must be willing to bury the dead. I like the way Robert Townsend says it *(Up The Organization,* pp. 75-76).

"It's about eleven times as easy to start something as it is to stop something. But ideas are good for a limited time—not forever.

"If Curtis Publishing had had a good V.P. in charge of killing things, the Saturday Evening Post, which was a great idea for many years, would have been killed before it ate up all those careers and all that capital.

"The internal-combustion engine should long

since have been killed and replaced with some form of external combustion (pollutionless) engine.

"General Foods, the AFL-CIO, the Bureau of the Budget, and the Ford Foundation should make it a practice to wipe out their worst product, service or activity every so often. And I don't mean cutting it back or remodeling it—I mean right between the eyes.

"And just to give us all a glimmer of light at the end of the tunnel, how about making it a matter of law that the federal government for the next hundred years will have to kill two old activities for each new one they start?"

May I suggest that we organize a committee to stop some of the foolishness going on in churches. As a church grows it should become more simple, not more complex. Bigness does not have to be equated with complexity. For several years now we have been working with our church constitution to make it simple. It was typically complex with the power in the hands of a few. The pastor was given the responsibility to appoint the music committee. He was the chairman of the missions committee. All that has been changed to spread out the authority and allow more people to minister in the Body.

We no longer accept people as members of Temple by "transfer of a letter." Where did that custom originate? The fact that one has been a member of a church in Podunckville may have nothing at all to do with his qualifications to be a member of Temple. So we require a personal testimony from every candidate who wants to join Temple. We do write the former church and inform it that the person has now joined our church, and they may wish to adjust their records accordingly. But the whole process of "church letters" is a poor way to conduct God's business if one believes the church consists of those who have experienced true conversion to Christ.

When I was forced home early from my vacation one year I took the opportunity to visit a new church in a neighboring community on Sunday. They were busily forming a new constitution. I was saddened at their approach. Their constitution was a conglomerate of several other traditional church constitutions. Their first draft was like most church constitutions with the exception of their reactions against the situation they had just left. A beautiful opportunity to organize for renewal at the beginning was being lost. We supplied preachers and leaders for that new church, and hopefully, we can help.

But this book is for the established church; one that has been in business for awhile and still is not experiencing renewal. Let me encourage you to believe that you can organize for change and expect change *now*.

A final suggestion is that anyone wanting to create change should continually reaffirm his orthodoxy. A basic reason that Christians in evangelical churches resist change is a fear that their leaders or the whole church are "going liberal." Christians don't want the "fundamentals" or "basics" touched.

That's good. But changing our methods must be distinguished from throwing the Bible out the window. Too often, *any* change is feared as "leaving our historic faith." I've tried to explain this phobia with a simple diagram. The words on your diagram will differ from mine, depending upon the semantics of your group.

**Theology**                                   **Methodology**

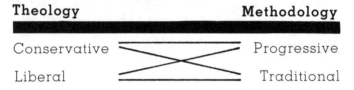

Conservative             Progressive

Liberal                    Traditional

The diagram shows two sets of terms. A conservative (or "fundamentalist," or "evangelical," or whatever label you use) in theology can be progressive or traditional in methodology. To tamper with methods is not to "lose our faith." This diagram often helps people. Once they realize that change does not affect their faith (except to give it a better vehicle of expression), they are willing to consider new ideas.

To sum up: Change can be created if it is introduced slowly, with a challenge, honestly, creatively, and by one who is a godly example and who reaffirms his orthodoxy.

# 9

# Compromise Is Not a Dirty Word

Dear brothers, you are only visitors here. Since your real home is in heaven I beg you to keep away from the evil pleasures of this world; they are not for you, for they fight against your very souls.

1 Peter 2:11 [TLB]

We are emerging from an era in which compromise ruined Christians, churches, and whole denominations. A few decades ago many of the mainline denominations began to compromise basic doctrines of Scripture. The Bible was traded for psychology textbooks by many who were supposed to be prophets of God. Many true Christians fought this kind of compromise and stayed within churches and denominations until they felt they had no impact, or were asked to leave. During those days many new denominations were created. Compromise brought dishonor to God, his Word, and his church. Compromise kept people from truth and from heaven.

Many Christians survived those denominational wars believing that compromise is a dirty word. Yet all of us compromise in many areas of life. The dictionary defines compromise as "a settlement in which each side gives up some demands or makes concessions."

Recently someone asked me if the love and unity of Temple had really been tested yet. At the time I couldn't think of any severe tests, except for some direct attacks by demons on certain church members. I mentioned that fact to the inquirer. Later, however, it struck me that Temple is frequently taking and passing tests that are potentially explosive to the unity of the church. The difference is that Christians at Temple are not "choosing up sides" for battle on issues. When disagreement arises, it is faced honestly, discussed, prayed over, and resolved.

Christians at Temple are willing to compromise with one another. No one gets his first choice all the time, so we learn to follow the rules of compromise. Sure, we've had disagreements about the color of new carpet, removal of a wall, singing of certain songs, use of the buildings, choice of words, order of services, and multitudes of other matters. But still we don't fight, argue, pout, or disrupt God's work. Emotionally mature people and groups make decisions in an orderly way. Willingness to compromise is part of Christian maturity. Compromise must be done with a smile, realizing that partial accomplishment is better than none.

Compromise simply means being willing to settle for less than the best in order to get the job done. Decisions must be made if progress is to be attained. We make decisions based on available data. In the area of politics, as you look at the slate of candidates you discover that none is perfect. Maybe none of the candidates exerts a positive Christian influence. Therefore, you do the best you can by voting for the ones who seem best to represent your particular political philosophy. That's better than not voting at all. You compromise by accepting less than the best.

On your job, even though you may have some problems, you generally don't quit. When you submit a requisition for so much of an item, but are offered less, you don't refuse to take *any*. You compromise and take what you get. When you ask for a raise of so much and are offered less, do you take it? Every sermon I preach is a compromise between

COMPROMISE IS NOT A DIRTY WORD    **95**

available time and my "purist" standards. I rarely meet my own standards for sermon preparation. I compromise and do the best I can in the time available.

If you have been married for any length of time you've discovered at least a few faults in your partner. Yet you don't throw away your marriage vows. You continue living and working with that person.

You compromise in your choice of churches. The church you belong to may be larger or smaller than you wish. It may not have an adequate young people's program or nursery facility. No matter what church you join, you compromise about something. That is preferable to not serving Christ through any church at all. Some wise man said, "If you ever find a perfect church, don't join it. You'll ruin it."

When you purchase a home or a car the salesman quotes a price. You offer less than that. You both realize that you will compromise before a price agreement can be reached. We compromise in many areas of life.

There were compromisers in the Bible. Paul was a compromiser. Paul never spoke against slavery. He wrote principles that made it wrong, yet he sent Onesimus to Philemon to continue as a slave. Paul told slaves to be good slaves. That was a compromise on his part. When Paul appealed to Caesar he was willing to stay in jail longer with a future chance of release. Paul accepted the sentence of guilt so he could make an appeal. A noncompromiser would have said, "I am innocent. Turn me loose." Paul compromised when he circumcised Timothy (Acts 16:1-3). In Acts 15 the Jerusalem council declared that non-Jewish believers did not have to be circumcised. The next chapter records Paul circumcising Timothy. That was a compromise. In Acts 21:17-26, Paul returned to Jerusalem and took a Jewish vow at the request of James and the church leaders. Again Paul obviously compromised his position.

Not only did Jewish customs cause Paul to compromise but so did heathen customs. In 1 Corinthians 8 he made it clear that there was nothing wrong with eating idol meat. Yet he told the Christians in Corinth not to do it if it offended a brother. That was a compromise of his position.

Elijah was a compromiser. In 2 Kings 5, Naaman, the Syrian general, was healed of leprosy because he obeyed the Word of the Lord through Elisha. In verses 15-17, Naaman offered a gift to Elisha which Elisha refused. Then the Syrian general declared that he was taking some dirt back to his home so that he, too, could worship Jehovah. In verse 19 Elisha said, "Go in peace." Elisha compromised his position. He didn't try to straighten Naaman out by telling him that soil from Israel wasn't necessary to worship God. A mature Christian can allow an immature Christian the privilege of mistakes in the process of growth.

A couple in our church had spent years looking for "truth." Don and Becky were in their early thirties and doing well in life, but they were unhappy.

Don had boxes of file folders crammed with notes from books, lectures, articles, and his own thinking about truth. He began to drink heavily, having already rejected Christianity as an option. Becky had been religious in her early life and had maintained an allegiance to a church, but had never experienced knowing Christ. Becky's first contact with Temple was through one of our members, as the two women chatted while swinging their children on the swings in a city park. A friendship developed, and Becky soon trusted Christ. Several months later Don received the Lord too. They started attending Temple regularly.

One evening this newborn couple was in our home and I mentioned the possibility of baptism. They were immediately up-tight. I gave them a booklet I've written on the subject and left the matter. They were not ready for baptism, so I compromised: I didn't push. A noncompromiser would have insisted that they do the scriptural thing now that they were true Christians. I let the matter drop.

Weeks later they expressed an interest in being baptized. I telephoned their home. Becky answered. I asked if they were interested. In icy tones Becky snapped that Don was, she definitely was not. I talked with Don and suggested we talk again later. After a few days, Becky called me. She was now ready, too. It was a thrill to baptize the couple.

The night of their baptism Becky told me that she would "never join Temple, or at least not for several years." I replied, "Fine. That's between you and God." I am convinced that Christians ought to join the local church. I strongly believe that. But I didn't tell Becky. I compromised. They both joined the next week—without one word from me or any person in the flesh. Compromise can be God's method.

God compromised with Israel and gave them a king against his perfect will (1 Samuel 8). God also compromised with Moses and did not blot out the nation for their sin. He only punished them.

Jesus compromised in the incarnation. He was willing to become man, talk with humans, and even die at the hands of evil men. Jesus paid taxes (Matthew 17:24-27). Does God owe man taxes? Certainly not. Jesus compromised his position. Jesus didn't speak against slavery. On one occasion he told his disciples, "I have many things to tell you but you can't bear them now." I interpret that to mean, "I will compromise and not tell you all the truth you really need."

In some areas we can't compromise. It's wrong to compromise clearly taught doctrines and absolutes of the Bible. We cannot compromise on the doctrines of the virgin birth, the inspiration of the Scriptures, and the necessity for individual salvation. We cannot compromise the fact that the Bible is the absolute authority with some absolute rules. It is never right to lie, cheat, steal, commit adultery. We should never compromise clear doctrines or absolutes.

Nor should convictions based on clear revelation

and clear principles be compromised. Even subjective convictions based on our background, teaching, or training should not be compromised if the compromise would harm us or make us feel guilty. This principle is found in 1 Corinthians 8. Paul said that although it is not wrong in general to eat idol meat, it would be wrong in certain cases. A weaker Christian might think he could eat idol meat, and then, having done it, might feel guilty. Paul said that this would make the brother stumble. The principle is that we are not to transgress our own convictions (even those not based on clearly taught principles of the Word) if it causes us to feel guilty. We should remember, however, that it is not wrong for these kinds of convictions to change.

In other areas we can compromise. We can compromise a lesser conviction for a greater one, but not a lesser absolute for a greater absolute. In other words I am not saying that it is ever okay to lie in order to love. If you have a conviction about a matter in your church and the church does otherwise, you should compromise your lesser conviction for the greater conviction you have about church unity. An elderly woman in our church came to me declaring that she was upset about our opening a coffeehouse to reach hard-core, counterculture young people. She said that she didn't believe in it and was opposed to it. But she concluded her remarks by saying, "Pastor, here is five dollars for that ministry." That's compromise in the right way.

We should compromise by being willing to work

with those who don't hold our convictions in order to continue working with them and influencing them. Paul worked with the Jews in the synagogue who did not hold his convictions. In one of our southern states I was once the pastor of a church which held a segregationist viewpoint. I compromised my position by not allowing black people to join that church, but I wouldn't compromise my position by keeping black people from worshiping in that church. I was willing to make the compromise so that I could continue working and influencing those believers for Jesus Christ. We are not called of God to straighten everyone out.

We should also compromise in the standards we want other people to live up to. In spite of the qualifications for deacons given in 1 Timothy 3, we do take less. Temple had an ideal of a perfect pastor, but they took less when they called me. Unless it's a clear violation of a scriptural absolute or principle, take what God gives you: compromise.

Several principles should guide us on the matter of compromise. First, remember that you might be wrong. In 2 Samuel 16, David was fleeing Jerusalem because his son Absalom was taking over the city with an army. On his way out of the city, Shimei cursed David and threw rocks at him. One of David's soldiers, Abishai, said, "David, let me remove his head." David said No in verse 10, declaring that God had told Shimei to do what he was doing. In chapter 19, David returned to Jerusalem after defeating Absalom, and Shimei met him at the river and apologized. Again Abishai wanted to remove his head, and again David denied him that privilege. David concluded by saying, "Now I know I am to be the king of Israel." David had some good indications that he was God's anointed king, yet he was not sure that he was always right or even that God was continuing to have his hand upon him. One reason people fail to see the scriptural principles about compromise is that they are always so sure they're right. I know I've been wrong at times.

Another principle is to remember that we all compromise in different areas. Don't be quick to condemn others. We can't crawl into the head of another person and know why he is doing what he is doing. It is difficult for us to know his convictions and background. Our tendency is to wrap our self-righteous robes around us when we see someone compromise in an area where we do not. We should resist that temptation.

A third principle is to balance the teaching of compromise with the teaching of separation in your own life. Don't use the teaching of compromise as an excuse for sin.

Compromise is not sin. It is God's method of progress. Many churches miss God's best because they aren't willing to allow progress in due course. The Christian and the church that must have purity "right now" in all areas of life usually end up discomfitted. The ones not willing to compromise and face reality become very frustrated. And frustrated Christians breed frustrated Christians, not spiritual

Christians. If you want renewal, be willing to accept its modest beginning. Don't "hold out" for the whole package all at once. Realize that any renewal must have a beginning, and accept small encouragements. Thank God for a little willingness to change shown by some of the pillars.

My first Sunday at Temple I decided that the beautiful wooden border on the top of the pulpit would have to go. Only my eyebrows peeked above that monster. I really wanted a whole new pulpit, but that decorative pulpit had been there much longer than I had. It fit into the motif and design of all the chancel furniture. But it was evidently designed by an architect who didn't want to see preachers, not by a preacher who wants to communicate with gestures and words. I compromised. I asked only that the top border be removed. The Board agreed. Renewal began. Now, several years later, I could burn the pulpit on the altar as an object lesson and probably get away with it. But the huge hulk still stands, simply because I haven't asked that it be replaced. And as far as renewal is concerned, its presence or absence is not an issue at all.

It is not right to do wrong in order to get a chance to do right. But it is right to do half-right in order to get a chance to do more right. And it is right to do things that are neither right nor wrong in order to get a chance to do right. Compromise is not a dirty word.

# 10

## God's Reputation

Of course, your former friends will be very surprised when you don't eagerly join them any more in the wicked things they do, and they will laugh at you in contempt and scorn.

1 Peter 4:4 [TLB]

After telling Christians that they should compromise, a balance must be established by warning that each Christian is responsible for God's reputation. There is no substitute for godly living. Progress, renewal, growth, and success are empty words to the church unless those words work in the context of walking close to God.

*"Indeed the idols I have loved so long*
*Have done my credit in this world much wrong,*
*Have drown'd my glory in a shallow cup*
*And sold my reputation for a song."*
　　　　　　　　*The Rubáiyát* of Omar Khayyám

The philosopher Syrus (42 B.C.) said, "A good reputation is more valuable than money." Another philosopher said, "It takes a lifetime to build a good reputation. It may be lost in a moment."

Your ideal is what you wish you were.

Your reputation is what people say you are.

Your character is what you are.

We must be very careful about this matter called reputation. Benjamin Franklin said, "Glass, china, and reputation are easily cracked and never well mended."

Each of us has a responsibility for the reputation of others. A parent has the responsibility for his children. Children have a responsibility for their parents. We are responsible for the reputation of our church. But more important is the fact that we are responsible for the reputation of God, for what others think about God. The Bible's word for the injury of God's reputation is blasphemy.

Injuring the reputation of God is so severe a sin that it is linked with the unpardonable sin in Matthew 12. In that chapter the Pharisees ascribed the work of Christ to Satan. The Pharisees had denied the clear revelation and conviction given them by the Holy Spirit, and in Matthew 12:31 they were accused of the unpardonable sin. An ultimate denial of revelation is still an unpardonable sin. One who dies without receiving Christ commits the unpardonable sin and no restitution can be made for him. To reject Christ is to injure the reputation of God's power to save and keep. One who dies with that blasphemy unforgiven will never be forgiven.

Strangely enough, in John 10, Jesus himself was accused of blasphemy, of injuring the reputation of God. Jesus had claimed equality with the Father. Jesus said, "Neither shall any man pluck them [my sheep] out of my hand" (John 10:28b), and "No man is able to pluck them out of my Father's hand" (John 10:29b). The intended equality of Father and Son was clear. In verse 30, Jesus made it even plainer when he said, "I and my Father are one." Then the Jews took up stones again to kill him. The penalty for blasphemy according to Leviticus 24:16 was death by stoning, a punishment administered only after a court trial.

The story in John 10 tells of a lynch mob trying to stone the Son of God, a frightful exhibition of human depravity. The accusation was clear. Jesus claimed to be God. Either he was God or he was a blasphemer. The Jews understood what Jesus was claiming. Jesus had only three ways to try to clear himself: (1) Prove that he never said these words, (2) Show that he meant something different by these words, or (3) Demonstrate that he is God.

Jesus clearly answered his accusers in this chapter by appealing to the Scriptures. In verses 34-36 he plainly showed them that he does claim to be God, and that they shouldn't be surprised at his claim. Then he appealed to their observation. Evil men had the audacity to believe they could catch God and harm him before his time. They failed but many believed, according to verse 42.

Jesus had demonstrated and said that he was deity. The Jews considered that affirmation to be harmful to God's reputation. They considered it blasphemous.

Blasphemy may be against God's person or God's power. The anti-Christ will blaspheme God, according to Revelation 13:6. The ungodly will blaspheme God during the tribulation, according to Revelation 17:3. Blaspheming may be directed against God's name, as in Romans 2:24, "The name of God is blasphemed among the Gentiles through you." Titus 2:5 says the Word of God is blasphemed; thus, those who deny the miracles of the Bible are blasphemers. Blasphemy may be against God's angels. Jude 8 says that evil people are "speaking evil of (Greek: "blaspheming") dignitaries (Greek: "angels")." Anyone who says that angels are not actively engaged in serving God is a blasphemer. Not only are atheists and agnostics blaspheming God, but so are religious people who deny the power and authority of God as revealed in the infallible Bible.

Jesus was blasphemed at his trial (Luke 22:64, 65). The soldiers denied that Jesus was God. The denial hurt the reputation of Jesus. Jesus was blasphemed on the cross (Mark 15:29, 30). They railed (Greek: "blasphemed") at him. The word is in the imperfect tense, which shows it was a repeated action. They doubted his person and power.

Remember, man can't harm the character of God. But man can injure the reputation of God, what others think about God, and that is blasphemy. Many people are reserving more punishment for themselves daily as they cast doubt upon God and his Word. If one chooses not to believe he will be punished forever. What if in addition he says things that cause others to doubt and disbelieve?

Part of blasphemy is casting doubt not only upon God and his Word but also upon his followers. Note that 1 Peter 4:4, 5 says, "In which they think it strange that you run not with them to the same profligacy, speaking evil of (Greek: "blaspheming") you: who shall give an account to him that is ready to judge the living and the dead." One who tries to hurt the reputation of a Christian who won't join him in sin is a blasphemer, and all blasphemy is ultimately against God.

We also need to know that Christians can blaspheme. Paul warned Christians, "Let all bitterness, and wrath, and anger, and clamor, and evil speaking (Greek: "blasphemy"), be put away from you, with all malice" (Ephesians 4:31). Believing false teaching is blasphemy, according to the Bible. The way of truth can be blasphemed by false teaching (2 Peter 2:2). Some Christians in Ephesus were teaching wrong doctrine. "And their word will eat as doth a gangrene: of whom are Hymenaeus and Philetus; who concerning the truth have erred, saying that the resurrection is past already; and overthrow the faith of some" (2 Timothy 2:17, 18). These two people are said to have held false doctrine. We find another word about one of these men back in 1 Timothy 1:20 when we read, "Of whom are Hymenaeus and Alexander; whom I have delivered unto Satan, that they may learn not to blaspheme." It is clear here that Hymenaeus was accused of blasphemy because he used or held wrong doctrine. The penalty was exclusion from fellowship.

Hymenaeus was cut off from fellowship and biblical teaching. Such exclusion leaves the believer without the strength and power he draws from other believers in the Body. It also leaves the believer open to temptation from Satan. If one persists in holding a wrong view of doctrine, that is blasphemy. That should scare us. We may hold on to wrong doctrine because we haven't really studied that doctrine. We may have taken the word of another and not the Word of God as our belief. This is the reason for systematic exposition at Temple.

Also Christians can cause others to blaspheme. Failure to be a good employee may cause someone to blaspheme God. "Let as many servants as are under the yoke count their own masters worthy of all honor that the name of God and his doctrine be not blasphemed" (1 Timothy 6:1). You see, your boss may look at your poor performance, and since he knows you are a Christian, may think, "Ha! Some Christian!" That hurts God's reputation. That is blasphemy. The same employer may also think poorly of your church if you are not doing your best on the job. Christians have a responsibility for each other and for the whole assembly. Others may blaspheme God because we don't act like Christians (Romans 2:21-24).

There is a special word to wives about blasphemy, "The aged women . . . may teach the young women to be sober minded, to love their husbands, to love their children, to be discreet, chaste, keepers at home, good, obedient to their own husbands, that the word of God be not blasphemed" (Titus 2:3-5). A Christian wife who is not obedient to her husband brings blasphemy upon God's Word. The church has a responsibility to help families. Biblical teaching on each family member's role will help Christians not to dishonor God. A woman who isn't discreet brings blasphemy upon God's Word. The Greek word translated *discreet* means "modest in dress." An immodest Christian woman harms the reputation of God. The Bible says so. Although we never harangue about short skirts at Temple, we do clearly expound these principles. The emphasis is not "list keeping" to prove one's spirituality, but a spiritual Christian will give attention to the teaching of God's Word. The Bible doesn't say how long, how short, how tight. But the mature Christian will be careful to be within the boundary of modest dress in his own context at a given time.

Secret sin may cause others to blaspheme God. Usually secret sin is not as secret as we wish. Remember David's sin with Bathsheba? David's sin caused God's enemies to blaspheme God (2 Samuel 12:14). Others were saying, "David does the same thing we do and he worships Jehovah." God's reputation was damaged.

This is the justification for church discipline. Christians living in open rebellion against God bring problems to the whole church. There have been occasions at Temple when I've had to talk with members about sin in their lives. I've tried to be kind and to explain that my purpose is not to judge or condemn, but to restore. I try to convey my own sadness that the member is missing God's best for his life, and that I want to help. When this approach doesn't work I must return to the Christian with another church leader and try again. If that doesn't help, the matter must be brought before the church and dismissal recommended. That hurts. It hurts the individual, the leaders, the whole church. But that is better than hurting God's reputation and the church's reputation by allowing willful blasphemy.

In summary, Christians blaspheme God in two

general ways. First, we doubt the power and involvement that God has in our lives. We have problems and frustrations, and we doubt that God is interested. Worry is a form of blasphemy. The Bible urges us to cast all our cares upon Christ, for he cares for us (1 Peter 5:7). We seldom say we doubt that God can help. We just act as if God isn't around. Our actions injure the reputation of God. Others look at our anxiety and conclude that our God isn't helping us at all. That damages God's reputation. That is blasphemy.

The biggest problem I have with myself and with others I counsel is waiting. Most Christians who are growing spiritually realize that God is in control, and that he will eventually work out the problem for his glory and our best interest. But when? That's the question. It's difficult to tell a wife whose husband is openly committing adultery just to "trust God" and not file for divorce. Certainly she is upset and doubts God. "Don't worry" is easy to say and hard to live. I tell seminarians, "Don't panic. God will place you in his service when you graduate." Many single adults want to marry. The word "wait" is ugly to them. But wait upon the Lord we must. Otherwise our worry casts long shadows upon God's name.

Second, we injure God's reputation when we identify with him but don't act right. We live the way the world lives. Some protest, "I can't always live right," and they are correct. No one can depend upon himself to live like a Christian. That means that we need God's power to help honor God with our lives. Only then will we be able to live like Christians and not be guilty of blasphemy. Again the importance of the daily devotional life is seen. Sitting under the Word can never be a substitute for being in the Word. Renewal is on its way when a group gets serious with God about living lives that make others admire the inner qualities of love and holiness. When Christians stop hurting God's reputation, God moves into the group and brings his blessing.

# 11

## The Future

**The end of the world is coming soon. Therefore be earnest, thoughtful men of prayer.**

1 Peter 4:7 [TLB]

Temple Baptist is not the perfect church. Many areas need improvement. Coordination is lacking in some areas. Communications are not always clear. Mistakes are made. Sometimes those in places of responsibility don't lead well and the ministry suffers. We have not arrived. We're just beginning, although the church is more than twenty years old. Renewal is here. We don't completely understand it, but we do enjoy it. I'm tempted sometimes to worry about the time when renewal may not be here. But I've realized that Temple is the normal church according to the New Testament. It may not be the usual church of today, but I sincerely believe that it's an example of New Testament normality. God is a Person of order. He operates according to prescribed principles. I've shared with you some principles I've learned.

The future looks exciting. Our facilities will probably hold us for another two years. We are looking for another church site now. Our plans are to grow to an attendance of 1,000 before attempting to start a new work. Observation of others has taught us that a new work often lacks the spirit of enthusiasm of the place where God is already blessing. We are not in favor of many small churches, struggling, fighting to pay the bills, and discouraged. We believe that one medium-sized church can have more of an impact on a community and more of a ministry to Christians than several small churches.

Temple is always exploring new possibilities for

ministry. We want our present ministries to grow deeper and larger, but we also desire that God will use us in new areas. Carolyn prayed for a ministry to the new neighbors who would inhabit the two vacant houses on each side of her home. Two "raw pagan" families, both considering divorces, moved in. Carolyn's prayer was answered, for she now has a significant ministry to those families. One of the women has become a Christian. Carolyn's contact with the wives began at the garbage cans where they took out their trash. We tease Carolyn about her invention of "trash can evangelism," but seriously, there are avenues of evangelism yet untouched. We want to be at the cutting edge of the field of evangelism.

We assume that a number of ministries will become lifeless and useless. I trust that our spiritual eyes will recognize God's time to bury those programs. Already the men of the church are forming teams to go to other churches to spread the principles of this book. They will go to a church and spend a weekend talking with that church's leaders and sharing with the whole church as the leaders determine. We aren't trying to win anyone over to anything. It's just that we have found these principles true and workable, and we're glad to share them with those who desire renewal.

One of our emphases in the future will be to follow Jesus, "who went about doing good" (Acts 10:38b). We want to do good in our community. We want the community to discover that we care. Our care is not a bribe to attend Temple. Our involvement is genuine. In the last few days I expressed my concern about a public issue to Mr. Paul Harvey, the national newscaster on ABC radio. He aired my concern to his listeners. I've talked with local YMCA leaders about cooperation in one of their projects. The deacons voted yesterday to pay a month's rent for a couple who just moved to town and had no money. There is no evidence that the family is Christian. They aren't church members, and may never be. One of our families had this family into their home for Thanksgiving. Another gave them additional food. Our Pioneer Girls participated as a group in last year's city cleanup day. Our four-wheel drivers helped take nurses to the hospitals during a violent snowstorm. Our young people have helped collect for the Heart Fund. Our children's choirs sing in nursing homes. We want to be known as people who do good.

Of course, we will continue to preach the gospel and teach the Word. We may not do it the way we've done it for the past three years. But the principles are set in concrete. Only the methods, the vehicles, will change. They must change. Renewal is needed. The results of renewal create a healthy, growing, spiritual, normal church.

It's happening at Temple. Temple was a dying church that refused to die. Wherever you are, whatever the health of your own local Body, remember:

*Renewal can happen in your church, too.*

**To him be glory and dominion for ever and ever. Amen**

(1 Peter 5:11).

# APPENDIX

## Sample Letters

**This letter is sent to every new resident in our city, enclosing a church brochure.**

Welcome to Colorado Springs.

Undoubtedly you are busily searching for businesses which handle merchandise and services that you need as a new resident. As a newcomer to our city you must have many needs. Usually new arrivals are looking for friends and something to do after they unpack.

Your arrival here probably means you have a certain amount of anxiety about your future in this area.

Have you ever considered that God has you here for a purpose? Your life in Colorado Springs could be the start of a wonderful adventure with God.

We would like to help you in your adjustments to our city. We would also consider it an honor if you would visit our church this Sunday and worship with us.

The enclosed brochure will tell you something about our church and where we are located.

If we can be of service to you, please call.

Sincerely,
Michael R. Tucker

This letter goes to those who will read Scripture at a morning service.

Dear _____

Would you please read Scripture and deliver the morning prayer at our service on the date indicated. If you cannot do so on the date indicated, please call Mrs. Cole at the church office and let her know. I'll call you the day before to give you the Scripture to read.

This is a very important part of the service so please give your careful consideration to the matter. May I suggest the following things about public Scripture reading and prayer.

### Scripture Reading

1. Read the passage several times before Sunday morning. At least one reading should be aloud.
2. Look up the pronunciation of words you are not sure of.
3. Try to understand the general idea of the passage.
4. Pay attention to commas and other punctuation.
5. On Sunday announce the passage and wait for the people to find it.
6. Read loudly and clearly and slowly.

### Prayer

1. Avoid generalities. "God bless the missionaries."
2. Don't try to impress with flowery phrases. You are talking to God, not the congregation.
3. Avoid repetition of phrases, even the repeated use of "Lord, Father, dear God."
4. Avoid clichés we all use so often in prayer.
5. Speak loudly and clearly (the organ may be playing softly).
6. Two to five minutes is adequate.
7. You may wish to organize your thoughts on paper or even write out your prayer, although it may not be best actually to read the prayer on Sunday.

8. Here are some items you may wish to include in your prayer:

a specific request for our missionary of the week

matters larger than our church—our president, a national need, a local tragedy

scriptural promises or words of encouragement from the Scriptures

the present service—I always appreciate prayer for the coming sermon

thanksgiving for God's grace in general (salvation, Word, freedom . . .)

thanksgiving for God's grace in specific (growth at Temple, recent blessings . . .)

Thank you,
Michael R. Tucker

This letter is sent to members who cooperate in our Family To Family Program.

Dear_____ _____:

Temple is growing very rapidly. It is becoming increasingly difficult to be sure that each new person has been truly welcomed into our homes as well as into our church.

The new Family to Family program at Temple has been initiated to help new folk become a part of our church family more easily, quickly, and thoroughly. As new individuals and families begin attending our church, members of Temple will be matched with them for the purpose of particularly befriending them during at least their first three months with us. Having them to your home for dinner and/or coffee, inviting them to extra activities at Temple as well as to all services, and helping them begin their children in their own age level groups are only a few suggestions as to how to implement the Family to Family relationship.

You have been chosen for a personal ministry with

_____

They live at _____ _____
and their phone number is _____ _____
Other information you might be interested in is

_____
_____
_____

Please contact one of us if you have any questions, or if for any reason you are not able to be a part of this ministry.

Within four weeks, would you let us know about your initial contact with this family, whether or not there is the possibility of a relationship being built, and how well acclimated to Temple this family is becoming.

Thank you so much,
Michael R. Tucker

This letter is typical of fifteen or twenty sent each week.

Dear_____:

I have just learned about (your accident, the death of your loved one, the tragedy in your family . . .), and I would like for you to know that there is comfort in Christ's presence.

God's love has made it possible for us to find peace of heart, even when our hearts are heavy. True peace, the peace which Jesus promised, is that inner serenity that persists when we are beset by turmoil and conflict.

God has promised to sustain us through periods of sorrow and disappointment so that we can more fully appreciate his love. May his Spirit encourage you during this time.

"Cast thy burden upon the Lord, and he shall sustain thee" (Psalm 55:22).

If we at Temple Baptist can do anything to help carry your burden at this time, please call. We are as close as your telephone and we want to help.

                                    Sincerely in Christ,
                                    Michael R. Tucker

P.S. The enclosed card may help you. Please read it.

# BIBLIOGRAPHY

William F. Arndt and F. Wilbur Gingrich, *Greek-English Lexicon of the New Testament and Other Early Christian Literature* (Grand Rapids: Zondervan, 1963)

Findley Edge, *The Greening of the Church* (Waco, Texas: Word Books, 1971)

William James, *The Principles of Psychology* (New York: Dover, 1918, 1950)

John Killinger, *The Centrality of Preaching* (Waco, Texas: Word Books, 1969)

Francis A. Schaeffer, *The Church at the End of the 20th Century* (Downers Grove, Illinois: Inter-Varsity Press, 1970)

Charles Haddon Spurgeon, *Lectures to My Students* (London: Marshall, Morgan and Scott, 1955)

*The Living Bible* (Wheaton, Illinois: Tyndale House Publishers, 1971)